singers on the yellow label

maria stader
elfride trötschel
annelies kupper
wolfgang windgassen
ernst haefliger
josef greindl
kim borg

discographies
compiled by
john hunt

contents

7	introduction
9	maria stader
69	elfride trötschel
91	annelies kupper
119	wolfgang windgassen
137	ernst haefliger
195	josef greindl
235	kim borg

Singers on the Yellow Label
Published by John Hunt.
Cover design by Richard Chluparty
© 2003 John Hunt
reprinted 2009
ISBN 978-1-901395-14-3

Sole distributors:
Travis & Emery,
17 Cecil Court,
London, WC2N 4EZ,
United Kingdom.
(+44) 20 7 459 2129.
sales@travis-and-emery.com

acknowledgement
these publications have been made possible by contributions or advance subscriptions from the following

Richard Ames
Stathis Arfanis
J.M. Blyth*
Edward Chibas*
Robert Dandois
Richard Dennis
Ronald Easdon
Henry Fogel*
Peter Fülop
Jean-Pierre Goossens
Alan Haine
Tadashi Hasegawa*
Bodo Igesz
Andrew Keener
Koji Kinoshita
Elisabeth Legge-Schwarzkopf*
John Mallinson*
Carlo Marinelli
Bruce Morrison
Alan Newcombe
Jim Parsons*
David Patmore*
James Pearson
Patrick Russell
Tom Scragg*
Robert Simmons
Michael Tanner
Nigel Wood*
Stephen Wright

Stefano Angeloni
Yoshihiro Asada
Brian Capon
George Cobby
Dennis Davis
John Derry
Hans-Peter Ebner*
Nobuo Fukumoto
Philip Goodman
Johann Gratz
Michael Harris*
Naoya Hirabayashi
E.M. Johnson
Rodney Kempster
Detlef Kissmann
Douglas MacIntosh
Neil Mantle
Philip Moores
W. Moyle
Hugh Palmer*
Laurence Pateman
J.A. Payne
Tully Potter
Ingo Schwarz
John Shackleton
Yoshihiko Suzuki*
Urs Weber*
Graeme Wright*
Ken Wyman

*indicates life subscriber

Singers on the yellow label: an introduction

These discographies follow on from the 1998 volume "Conductors on the yellow label", which focussed on the conducting talents used by the Deutsche Grammophon Gesellschaft to re-establish itself on the world's record markets after Germany's defeat in World War II. As the period in question stretches from around 1949 until the early 1960s, we are basically concerned with the early years of the 12inch (30cm) long-playing record, although a fair proportion of the market was still devoted to 10inch (25cm) records which were more reasonably priced for impecunious collectors, not to mention shellac discs playing at 78rpm (with both standard and extended playing time, the latter being a peculiarity to Deutsche Grammophon and its associate labels) and extended playing 45rpm vinyl discs (commonly known as EPs). From around 1959 stereophonic versions of many of the new LPs and EPs appeared on the market alongside the previous mono editions.

As far as female voices are concerned, we are still with a generation who remained securely within their *Fach* and who recorded parts from the opera and concert repertory which was theirs on stage. There was the lyric soprano *Elfride Trötschel* with parts like Mozart's Susanna, Puccini's Mimi and Dvorak's Rusalka, and the youthful dramatic *Annelies Kupper* with numerous parts from Richard Strauss, Mozart's Donna Anna, Verdi's Aida and Desdemona and Giordano's Maddalena di Coigny. It seems to me rather unfair that neither of these vocalists are mentioned in encyclopaedias of twentieth-century singers by experts like John Steane and Jürgen Kesting. On the evidence of recordings now re-issued on compact disc, they are worthy successors to more illustrious predecessors in their range like *Maria Cebotari* or *Viorica Ursuleac*. One of the earliest examples of a record company cultivating a "gramophone" voice was with *Maria Stader*, essentially a lyric concert and Mozart singer who is heard, apart from in arias by Lortzing and Nicolai which fit her voice like a glove, in selections from Madama Butterfly and La Traviata - parts into which she would scarcely have ventured on stage, even if her small physique had permitted.

Stader's parallel among male voices on DG's roster was the tenor *Ernst Haefliger* (like her he was also a Swiss-Hungarian). Like his predecessor and teacher *Julius Patzak*, he was a stylist *par excellence* in gramophone parts like Beethoven's Florestan and Offenbach's Hoffmann, although his greatest contributions to the catalogues are probably his Mozart opera and concert parts as well as the oratorios of Bach and Handel. Quite a different tenor voice was *Wolfgang Windgassen*, starting his career as Mozart's Tamino but developing, with encouragement from Wieland Wagner and the record companies, into a Wagnerian all-rounder. Most of the DG Wagner extracts in which Windgassen participated actually pre-date his main successes in the major roles both at Bayreuth and internationally – there his regular partners were Birgit Nilsson, Astrid Varnay and Martha Mödl. A basic dryness of tone was compensated for with a fine sense of pacing and a heightened feeling for the text. Also established in the Wagnerian mainstream was the bass *Josef Greindl*, although his stage repertoire embraced performances of Russian and Italian parts (Boris Godunov, Philipp II). He took up several pieces by Carl Orff, and was something of a specialist in the ballads of Carl Loewe. The last singer in our survey was *Kim Borg*, forerunner of later Finnish basses *Martti Talvela* and *Matti Salminen*. Borg was a fine Lieder singer as well as being used by DG in countless opera highlight LPs, ranging from Mozart to Puccini.

On the subject of opera highlights, it is interesting to note that in the period under review these tended to be recorded piecemeal rather than as entities, so that individual arias or ensembles could also be issued on individual 78s or EPs and on artist portrait LPs (often in 10inch format). These were often recorded in the original language for the international market and in German for domestic issue.

It was in the case of the Wagnerians in our list that I realised it was necessary to include mention of the singers' recordings for other companies, and I have extended this to all the others covered, including the wealth of live broadcasts which have proliferated, both officially and unofficially, since the 1970s. There are doubtless gaps still to be filled here, and I am always glad to hear from collectots who can add to the infomation which I have listed.

My special thanks goes to Alan Newcombe of DG in Hamburg, who has looked up many recording dates for me, both for this volume and for many of my past discographies. Others who have helped with information include Richard Chlupaty, Syd Gray, Bill Holland and Roderick Krüsemann.

John Hunt   Copyright 2003

maria stader
1911-1999

JOHANN SEBASTIAN BACH (1685-1750)

cantata no 51 "jauchzet gott in allen landen"
munich	*soprano soloist*	lp: dg archiv APM 14 144/SAPM 198 027
18-21	**k.richter**	cd: dg 435 1422/439 3872
august	munich bach	
1959	orchestra	

cantata no 202 "weichet nur betrübte schatten"
munich	*soprano soloist*	lp: dg archiv APM 14 144/SAPM 198 027
15-21	**k.richter**	
august	munich bach	
1959	orchestra	

maria stader also sang cantata no 57 "selig ist der mann" for concert hall record club, conducted by jean-marie auberson; and cantatas nos 199 "mein herze schwimmt in blut" and 209 "non sa che sia dolore" for the pelca label, conducted by helmut müller-brühl

johannes-passion, excerpt (zerfliesse mein herze)
munich	**k.richter**	lp: dg 135 103
may	munich bach	cd: dg 447 3342
1961	orchestra	

magnificat
munich	*soprano soloist*	lp: dg archiv AP 13 078/APM 14 197/
april	**k.richter**	SAP 195 078/SAPM 198 197/
1961	munich bach	2722 018
	orchestra	cd: dg 419 4662/463 7012
	and chorus	
	töpper	
	haefliger	
	fischer-dieskau	

maria stader also sang this part in recordings of the magnificat for concert hall record club conducted by jean-marie auberson and for nixa conducted by walter reinhart: the reinhart version was also subsequently issued by concert hall and by musical masterpiece society

LANGSPIELPLATTE 33

ARCHIV PRODUKTION
DES MUSIKHISTORISCHEN STUDIOS DER DEUTSCHEN GRAMMOPHON GESELLSCHAFT

IX. FORSCHUNGSBEREICH
Das Schaffen Johann Sebastian Bachs
SERIE A · KANTATEN

„Jauchzet Gott in allen Landen"
Kantate am 15. Sonntag nach Trinitatis, BWV 51

„Weichet nur, betrübte Schatten"
Hochzeitskantate, BWV 202

Maria Stader, Sopran
Willi Bauer, Trompete · Kurt Hausmann, Oboe
Otto Büchner, Violine
Fritz Henker, Fagott · Hedwig Bilgram, Cembalo
Münchener Bach-Orchester
Dirigent: Karl Richter

IX. FORSCHUNGSBEREICH, SERIE A · J. S. BACH, KANTATEN „JAUCHZET GOTT IN ALLEN LANDEN" / „WEICHET NUR, BETRÜBTE SCHATTEN"   14144 APM

mass in b minor
munich	*soprano soloist*	lp: dg archiv APM 14 190-14 192/
february-	**k.richter**	SAPM 198 190-198 192/2710 001/
april	munich bach	2722 017/2723 065
1961	orchestra	cd: dg 427 1552
	and chorus	*excerpts*
	töpper	lp: dg LPEM 19 300/SLPEM 136 300/
	haefliger	2533 313
	engen	

matthäus-passion, excerpts (ich will dir mein herze schenken; aus liebe will mein heiland sterben)
munich	**k.richter**	lp: dg 135 103
may	munich bach	cd: dg 447 3342
1961	orchestra	

LUDWIG VAN BEETHOVEN (1770-1827)

missa solemnis
berlin	*soprano soloist*	lp: dg LPM 18 224-18225/
3-12	**böhm**	LPM 18 232-18 233
january	berlin	lp: dg heliodor 89 679-89 680
1955	philharmonic	lp: decca (usa) DX 135
	saint hedwig's	cd: dg 449 7372
	choir	*also unofficially issued in an incorrectly dated lp*
	radev	*edition by discocorp*
	dermota	
	greindl	

maria stader also sang the soprano solo part in a recording of beethoven symphony no 9 "choral" for concert hall record club, conducted by willem van otterloo; the role of marzelline in a complete recording of fidelio for westminster, conducted by hans knappertsbusch; and soprano soloist in the orarorio "christus am ölberge", also for westminster and conducted by hermann scherchen

GEORGES BIZET (1838-1875)

carmen, excerpt (je dis que rien ne m'épouvante)
berlin 17 may 1954	*role of micaela* **könig** rso berlin	45: dg EPL 30 291
berlin 17 may 1954	**könig** rso berlin *sung in german*	45: dg EPL 30 290
munich 6-12 january 1958	**fricsay** bavarian state orchestra *sung in german*	lp: dg LPEM 19 153/LPEM 19 191/ SLPEM 136 032/2535 297 cd: dg 447 8092

carmen, excerpt (parle-moi de ma mere)
munich 6-12 january 1958	*role of micaela* **fricsay** bavarian state orchestra simandy *sung in german*	lp: dg LPEM 19 153/LPEM 19 191/ SLPEM 136 032/2535 297 cd: dg 447 8092

JOHANNES BRAHMS (1833-1897)

ein deutsches requiem
berlin 28 january- 6 february 1955	*soprano soloist* **lehmann** berlin philharmonic saint hedwig's choir motettenchor wiener	lp: dg LPM 18 238-18 239/ LPM 18 258-18 259 lp: dg heliodor 89 696-89 697 lp: decca (usa) DX 136 cd: dg 457 7102 *recording completed in may 1955*

maria stader also took this part in a stuttgart radio recording conducted by carl schuricht and published by archiphon and trésor

stader 17

ANTON BRUCKNER (1824-1896)

mass no 3
munich	*soprano soloist*	lp: dg LPM 18 829/SLPM 138 829/
4-6	**jochum**	2720 054
july	bavarian radio	cd: dg 423 1272/447 4092
1962	orchestra	*excerpts*
	and chorus	lp: dg LPEM 19 491/SLPEM 136 491
	hellmann	
	haefliger	
	borg	

te deum
berlin	*soprano soloist*	lp: dg SLPEM 136 552/139 117-139 118/
28 june-	**jochum**	139 999/2707 026/2720 054/
2 july	berlin	2740 136
1965	philharmonic	cd: dg 423 1272/457 7432
	deutsche oper	
	chorus	
	wagner	
	haefliger	
	lagger	

maria stader also sang the soprano solo part in a recording of bruckner te deum for american columbia, conducted by eugene ormandy

psalm 150
berlin	*soprano soloist*	lp: dg 139 137-139 138/139 999/
28 june-	**jochum**	2707 005/2720 054
2 july	berlin	cd: dg 423 1272/457 7432
1965	philharmonic	
	deutsche oper	
	chorus	

GLUCK
ORPHÉE ET EURYDICE

DIETRICH FISCHER-DIESKAU
MARIA STADER • RITA STREICH
ORCHESTRE SYMPHONIQUE DE LA RADIO DE BERLIN
FERENC FRICSAY

Deutsche Grammophon

DOUBLE
2 CD

ANTONIN DVORAK (1841-1904)

requiem
prague	*soprano soloist*	lp: dg LPM 18 547-18 548/
30 january-	**ancerl**	SLPM 138 026-138 027/2707 005
4 february	czech	cd: dg 437 3772
1959	philharmonic	*probably also published on the supraphon label*
	orchestra	
	and chorus	
	wagner	
	haefliger	
	borg	

CHRISTOPH WILLIBALD GLUCK (1714-1787)

orfeo ed euridice
berlin	*role of euridice*	lp: dg LPM 18 343-18 344/
8-12	**fricsay**	LPM 18 345-18 346/2700 103
september	rso berlin	cd: dg 439 7112
1956	rias choir	
	streich	
	fischer-dieskau	
	sung in german	

CHARLES GOUNOD (1818-1893)

faust, excerpt (il était un roi de thulé)
munich	*role of marguérite*	45: dg NL 32 068
25-26	**leitner**	
april	munich	
1954	philharmonic	

munich	**leitner**	45: dg NL 32 067
25-26	munich	
april	philharmonic	
1954	*sung in german*	

faust, excerpt (o dieu que de bijoux!/ah je ris!)
munich	*role of marguérite*	45: dg NL 32 068/EPL 30 474
25-26	**leitner**	
april	munich	
1954	philharmonic	

munich	**leitner**	45: dg NL 32 067
25-26	munich	lp: dg LPEM 19 095
april	philharmonic	lp: dg heliodor 89 651
1954	*sung in german*	

faust, excerpt (il se fait tard)
munich	*role of marguérite*	lp: dg LPEM 19 095
10 january	**leitner**	lp: dg heliodor 89 651
1957	munich	
	philharmonic	
	hoppe	
	sung in german	

faust, excerpt (par ici mes amis!)
munich	*role of marguérite*	45: dg EPL 30 474
8 january	**leitner**	lp: preiser PR 135013
1957	munich	
	philharmonic	
	naaff	
	wächter	

munich	**leitner**	45: dg EPL 30 238
8 january	munich	lp: dg LPEM 19 095
1957	philharmonic	lp: dg heliodor 89 651
	naaff	
	wächter	
	sung in german	

faust, excerpt (alerte! alerte!)
munich	*role of marguérite*	lp: dg LPEM 19 095
11-12	**leitner**	lp: dg heliodor 89 651
january	munich	
1957	philharmonic	
	bavarian radio	
	chorus	
	hoppe	
	borg	
	sung in german	

roméo et juliette, excerpt (je veux vivre dans ce reve)
munich	*role of juliette*	45: dg NL 32 147
4 november	**ludwig**	
1955	munich	
	philharmonic	

munich	**ludwig**	45: dg NL 32 146
4 november	munich	lp: dg LPE 17 088
1955	philharmonic	
	sung in german	

GEORGE FRIDERIC HANDEL (1685-1759)

brockes-passion
basel	*soprano soloist*	lp: dg archiv APM 14 418-14 420/
26 june-	**wenzinger**	SAPM 198 418-198 420/
9 july	schola cantorum	2710 006/413 9221
1961	basiliensis	cd: dg archiv 463 6442
	regensburg	*excerpts*
	cathedral choir	45: dg archiv EPA 37 223/SEPA 102 223
	moser	
	esswood	
	haefliger	
	jennings	
	adam	
	stämpfli	

joshua, excerpt (o had i jubal's lyre!)
munich	*soprano soloist*	lp: dg 135 103
may	**k.richter**	cd: dg 447 3342
1961	munich bach	
	orchestra	
	sung in german	

messiah, excerpts (he shall feed his flock; i know that my redeemer liveth)
munich	*soprano soloist*	lp: dg 135 103
may	**k.richter**	cd: dg 447 3342
1961	munich bach	
	orchestra	
	sung in german	

maria stader also sang in a berlin radio performance of judas maccabaeus conducted by ferenc fricsay and published by melodram

FRANZ JOSEF HAYDN (1732-1809)

die jahreszeiten
berlin	*soprano soloist*	lp: dg 2721 170
11 november	**fricsay**	*recorded at a public concert*
1961	rso berlin	
	saint hedwig's choir	
	haefliger	
	greindl	

die jahreszeiten, excerpts (willkommen jetzt; welch' labung für die sinne)
munich	*soprano soloist*	lp: dg 135 063
may	**k.richter**	cd: dg 447 3342
1961	munich bach orchestra	

nelson mass
budapest	*soprano soloist*	lp: dg LPEM 19 195/SLPEM 139 195
20-23	**ferencsik**	*probably also published on the hungaroton label*
june	hungarian state orchestra and chorus	
1966	hellmann	
	haefliger	
	halem	

saint cecilia mass
munich	*soprano soloist*	lp: dg LPM 18 545-18 546/
10-12	**jochum**	SLPM 138 028-138 029
october	bavarian radio	cd: dg 437 3832/445 0522
1958	orchestra	*excerpts*
	and chorus	lp: dg LPEM 19 491/SLPEM 136 491
	höffgen	
	holm	
	greindl	

die schöpfung, excerpts (nun beut die flur; auf starkem fittiche)
munich	*soprano soloist*	lp: dg 135 063
may	**k.richter**	cd: dg 447 3342
1961	munich bach	
	orchestra	

ALBERT LORTZING (1801-1851)

der wildschütz, excerpt (auf des lebens raschen wogen)
munich	*role of baronin*	45: dg EPL 30 114
3 november	**ludwig**	lp: dg LPE 17 088
1955	munich	
	philharmonic	

GUSTAV MAHLER (1860-1911)

maria stader is soprano soloist in performances of the second symphony conducted by sir john barbirolli published by testament, and of the fourth symphony conducted by bruno walter and published by nuovo era

JULES MASSENET (1842-1912)

manon, excerpt (adieu notre petite table)
munich	*role of manon*	78: dg LV 36 119
21-24	**leitner**	45: dg NL 32 060
april	munich	
1954	philharmonic	

munich	**leitner**	45: dg NL 32 059
21-24	munich	lp: dg LPE 17 088
april	philharmonic	
1954	*sung in german*	

manon, excerpt (je marche sur tous les chemins)
munich	*role of manon*	78: dg LV 36 119
21-24	**leitner**	45: dg NL 32 060
april	munich	
1954	philharmonic	

munich	**leitner**	45: dg NL 32 059
21-24	munich	lp: dg LPE 17 088
april	philharmonic	
1954	*sung in german*	

FELIX MENDELSSOHN-BARTHOLDY (1809-1847)

elijah, excerpt (hear ye israel!)
munich   *soprano soloist*   lp: dg 135 063
may   **k.richter**   cd: dg 447 3342
1961   munich bach
                orchestra
                sung in german

es weiss und rät es doch keiner
munich   engel, piano   lp: dg LPEM 19 136
october   cd: dg 447 3342
1957

nachtlied (vergangen ist der lichte tag)
munich   engel, piano   lp: dg LPEM 19 136
october   cd: dg 447 3342
1957

neue liebe (in dem mondenscheine im walde)
munich   engel, piano   lp: dg LPEM 19 136
october   cd: dg 447 3342
1957

schilflied (auf dem teich dem regungslosen)
munich   engel, piano   lp: dg LPEM 19 136
october   cd: dg 447 3342
1957

wanderlied (laue luft kommt blau geflossen)
munich   engel, piano   lp: dg LPEM 19 136
october   cd: dg 447 3342
1957

WOLFGANG AMADEUS MOZART

Die Entführung aus dem Serail

Maria Stader · Rita Streich
Ernst Haefliger
Martin Vantin
Josef Greindl
Dirigent: Ferenc Fricsay

Deutsche Grammophon Gesellschaft

WOLFGANG AMADEUS MOZART (1756-1791)

don giovanni
berlin	*role of elvira*	lp: dg LPM 18 580-18 582/
september-	**fricsay**	SLPM 138 050-138 052/
october	rso berlin	2728 003/2730 014
1958	rias choir	cd: dg 437 3412/463 6292
	jurinac	
	seefried	
	haefliger	
	fischer-dieskau	
	kohn	
	kreppel	
	sardi	

don giovanni, excerpts (vedrai carino; batti batti)
berlin	*role of zerlina*	45: dg EPL 30 266
18-22	**fricsay**	cd: dg 447 3342
january	rso berlin	
1957	*sung in german*	

die entführung aus dem serail
berlin	*role of konstanze*	lp: dg LPM 18 197-18 198/
16-24	**fricsay**	LPM 18 184-18 185/2700 010/
may	rso berlin	2730 014
1954	rias choir	lp: dg heliodor 89 756-89 757
	streich	lp: decca (usa) DX 133
	haefliger	cd: dg 437 7302/445 4122
	vantin	*excerpts*
	greindl	lp: dg LPE 17 027/LPEM 19 409
		cd: dg 435 3182/447 3342

idomeneo, excerpts (zeffiretti lusinghieri; se il padre perdei)
salzburg *role of ilia* lp: dg LPEM 19 369/SLPEM 136 369
april **paumgartner** cd: dg 435 3182
1962 camerata
 academica

le nozze di figaro
berlin *role of contessa* lp: dg LPM 18 697-18 699/
12-22 **fricsay** SLPM 138 697-138 699/
september rso berlin 2728 004/2730 014
1960 rias choir cd: dg 437 6712
 seefried *excerpts*
 töpper lp: dg LPEM 19 272/SLPEM 136 272
 cappecchi
 fischer-dieskau

le nozze di figaro, excerpts (porgi amor; dove sono)
berlin *role of contessa* lp: dg LPEM 19406/SLPEM 136 406/
12-14 **leitner** 2535 279
december berlin cd: dg 423 8742/435 3182
1961 philharmonic
 sung in german

le nozze di figaro, excerpt (che soave zeffiretto)
berlin *role of contessa* lp: dg LPEM 19 406/SLPEM 136 406/
12-14 **leitner** 2535 279
december berlin cd: dg 423 8742/435 3182
1961 philharmonic
 streich
 sung in german

le nozze di figaro, excerpt (deh vieni non tardar)
berlin *role of susanna* 45: dg EPL 30 266
18-22 **fricsay**
january rso berlin
1957 *sung in german*

le nozze di figaro, excerpt (non so piu)
munich	*role of cherubino*	45: dg NL 32 125
1 november	**ludwig**	cd: dg 447 3342
1955	bavarian radio orchestra	

munich	**ludwig**	45: dg NL 32 124
1 november	bavarian radio	lp: dg LPEM 19 066
1955	orchestra	lp: dg heliodor 89 539
	sung in german	

le nozze di figaro, excerpt (voi che sapete)
munich	*role of cherubino*	45: dg NL 32 125
1 november	**ludwig**	lp: dg LPM 18 558-18 559
1955	bavarian radio orchestra	cd: dg 447 3342

munich	**ludwig**	45: dg NL 32 124
1 november	bavarian radio	lp: dg LPEM 19 066
1955	orchestra	lp: dg heliodor 89 539
	sung in german	

maria stader also recorded the two cherubino arias for hmv switzerland

il re pastore, excerpts (aer tranquillo; barbaro o dio!; alla selva al prato)
salzburg	*role of aminta*	lp: dg LPEM 19 369/SLPEM 136 369
april	**paumgartner**	cd: dg 435 3182
1962	camerata academica	

maria stader also recorded the aria l'amero saro costante from il re pastore for hmv

die zauberflöte
berlin	*role of pamina*	lp: dg LPM 18 264-18 266/
june	**fricsay**	LPM 18 267-18 269/2728 009
1955	rso berlin	lp: dg heliodor 89 662-89 664/
	rias choir	2701 003/2730 014
	streich	lp: decca (usa) DX 134
	otto	lp: philips 6747 387
	schech	lp: eterna 820 226-820 228
	klose	cd: dg 435 7412/459 4972
	haefliger	*excerpts*
	vantin	45: dg EPL 30 237
	fischer-dieskau	lp: dg LPEM 19 194
	greindl	lp: decca (usa) DL 9932
	borg	cd: dg 447 3342

a questo seno deh vieni, concert aria
munich	**ludwig**	45: dg EPL 30 223
2 november	bavarian radio	cd: dg 447 3342
1955	orchestra	

alma grande e nobil core, concert aria
munich	**lehmann**	45: dg EPL 30 458
2-3	bavarian radio	lp: dg LPM 18 219
october	orchestra	cd: dg 447 3342
1954		

chi sa chi sa qual sia, concert aria
salzburg	**paumgartner**	lp: dg LPEM 19 369/SLPEM 136 369
april	camerata	cd: dg 435 3182
1962	academica	

misera dove son, concert aria
munich	**lehmann**	45: dg EPL 30 458
2-3	bavarian radio	lp: dg LPM 18 219
october	orchestra	cd: dg 447 3342
1954		

nehmt meinen dank, concert aria
salzburg	**paumgartner**	lp: dg LPEM 19 369/SLPEM 136 369
april	camerata	cd: dg 435 3182
1962	academica	

maria stader also recorded this concert aria for hmv

un moto di gioia, concert aria
munich	**ludwig**	45: dg EPL 30 223
2 november	bavarian radio	cd: dg 447 3342
1955	orchestra	

voi avete un cor fedele, concert aria
salzburg	**paumgartner**	lp: dg LPEM 19 369/SLPEM 136 369
april	camerata	cd: dg 435 3182
1962	academica	

maria stader also recorded this concert aria for hmv, and in a canadian television recording conducted by sir thomas beecham published by video artists international

vorrei spiegarvi o dio, concert aria
salzburg	**paumgartner**	lp: dg LPEM 19 369/SLPEM 136 369
april	camerata	cd: dg 435 3182
1962	academica	

maria stader also recorded this concert aria for hmv, and in a canadian television recording conducted by sir thomas beecham published by video artists international
maria stader also recorded the concert aria per pieta bell' idol mio for hmv

mass in c minor
berlin	*soprano soloist*	lp: dg LPM 18 624/SLPM 138 124
30 september-	**fricsay**	cd: dg 429 1612/437 3892/463 6122
1 october	rso berlin	*excerpts*
1959	saint hedwig's choir	lp: dg LPEM 19 291/SLPEM 136 281
	töpper	
	haefliger	
	sardi	

maria stader also recorded the mass for concert hall record club, conducted by jean-marie auberson

et incarnatus est/mass in c minor

berlin	*soprano soloist*	lp: dg LPE 17 110
12-14	**könig**	cd: dg 435 1422/437 3832
november	rso berlin	
1957		

coronation mass

berlin	*soprano soloist*	lp: dg LP 16 096/LPE 17 141/
18-21	**markevitch**	LPX 29 330
february	berlin	lp: decca (usa) DL 9805
1954	philharmonic	cd: dg 437 3832
	saint hedwig's	
	choir	
	wagner	
	krebs	
	greindl	

paris	**markevitch**	lp: dg LPE 17 222/LPM 18 631/
7-8	lamoureux	SLPE 133 222/SLPM 138 131/
december	orchestra	136 511/2535 148
1959	brasseur choir	cd: dg 429 5102/457 7442
	dominguez	*excerpts*
	haefliger	lp: dg LPEM 19 491/SLPEM 136 491
	roux	

exsultate jubilate, motet

berlin	**fricsay**	78: dg LVM 72 473
january	rso berlin	45: dg EPL 30 082
1954		lp: dg LPE 17 027/LPM 18 554-18 555
		lp: decca (usa) DX 132
		cd: dg 457 7302

berlin	**fricsay**	45: dg EPL 30 595/SEPL 121 595
3-4	rso berlin	lp: dg LPEM 19 291/SLPEM 136 281/
june		136 511/2535 148/2535 712/
1960		2705 005
		cd: dg 435 1422/437 3832/
		439 4122/447 3342

maria stader also recorded the alleluja from exsultate jubilate for hmv

agnus dei/litaniae lauretanae k195
berlin	**könig**	lp: dg LPE 17 110
12-14	rso berlin	cd: dg 435 1422/437 3832
november	rias choir	
1957		

laudate dominum/vesperae de dominica k321
berlin	**könig**	lp: dg LPE 17 110
12-14	rso berlin	cd: dg 435 1422/437 3832
november		
1957		

maria stader also recorded these complete vespers for concert hall record club, conducted by walter reinhart

laudate dominum/vesperae solennes de confessore k339
berlin	**könig**	lp: dg LPE 17 110
12-14	rso berlin	cd: dg 435 1422/437 3832
november	rias choir	
1957		

berlin	**fricsay**	lp: dg LPEM 19 291/SLPEM 136 281
june	rso berlin	cd: dg 447 3342
1960	rias choir	

maria stader also sings laudate dominum in an unpublished bavarian radio recording conducted by eugen jochum

maria stader also recorded ora pro nobis from regina coeli k108 for hmv, and in an unpublished bavarian radio recording conducted by eugen jochum

maria stader also recorded the soprano part in mozart requiem mass for telefunken conducted by karl richter, and in an austrian radio recording conducted by carl schuricht and published by archiphon and trésor

maria stader also recorded a group of mozart lieder for westminster, accompanied by jörg demus

OTTO NICOLAI (1810-1849)

die lustigen weiber von windsor, excerpt (nun eilt herbei!)
munich	*role of frau fluth*	45: dg EPL 30 114
17 may	**leitner**	lp: dg LPE 17 088/LPEM 19049
1955	munich	lp: dg heliodor 89 648
	philharmonic	lp: decca (usa) DL 9839

die lustigen weiber von windsor, excerpt (nein das ist wirklich doch zu keck!)
munich	**leitner**	lp: dg LPEM 19 049
17 may	munich	lp: dg heliodor 89 648
1955	philharmonic	lp: decca (usa) DL 9839
	klose	

GIACOMO PUCCINI (1858-1924)

la boheme, excerpt (si mi chiamano mimi)
berlin	*role of mimi*	45: dg EPL 30 291
16 may	**könig**	
1957	rso berlin	

berlin	**könig**	45: dg EPL 30 290
16 may	rso berlin	
1957	*sung in german*	

madama butterfly, excerpt (ecco la vetta)
munich	*role of butterfly*	lp: dg LPE 17 017
8-11	**hollreiser**	
june	munich	
1954	philharmonic	
	bavarian opera	
	chorus	

munich	**hollreiser**	lp: dg LPE 17 016
8-11	munich	
june	philharmonic	
1954	bavarian opera	
	chorus	
	sung in german	

madama butterfly, excerpt (un bel di vedremo)
munich	*role of butterfly*	lp: dg LPE 17 017
8-11	**hollreiser**	
june	munich	
1954	philharmonic	

munich	**hollreiser**	lp: dg LPE 17 016
8-11	munich	
june	philharmonic	
1954	*sung in german*	

madama butterfly, excerpt (scuoti quella fronda di ciliegio)
munich	*role of butterfly*	lp: dg LPE 17 017
8-11	**hollreiser**	
june	munich	
1954	philharmonic	
	töpper	

munich	**hollreiser**	lp: dg LPE 17 016
8-11	munich	
june	philharmonic	
1954	töpper	
	sung in german	

madama butterfly, excerpt (quest' obi pomposa di scoglier mi tarda/ bimba dagli occhi)
munich	*role of butterfly*	lp: dg LPE 17 017
8-11	**hollreiser**	
june	munich	
1954	philharmonic	
	van dijk	

munich	**hollreiser**	lp: dg LPE 17 016
8-11	munich	
june	philharmonic	
1954	van dijk	
	sung in german	

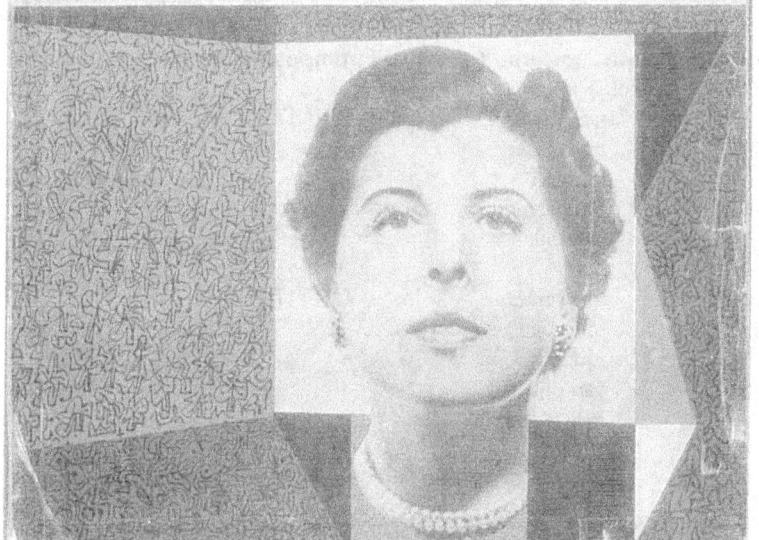

turandot, excerpt (signore ascolta)
berlin	*role of liu*	45: dg EPL 30 470
15 may	**könig**	
1957	rso berlin	

berlin	**könig**	45: dg EPL 30 469
12 may	rso berlin	
1957	*sung in german*	

turandot, excerpt (tu che di gel sei cinta)
berlin	*role of liu*	45: dg EPL 30 470
15 may	**könig**	
1957	rso berlin	

berlin	**könig**	45: dg EPL 30 469
12 may	rso berlin	
1957	*sung in german*	

GIOACCHINO ROSSINI (1792-1868)

stabat mater
berlin	*soprano soloist*	lp: dg LPM 18 203-18 204/LPM 18 340/
16-19	**fricsay**	2535 718
september	rso berlin	lp: dg heliodor 89 610/2548 126
1954	rias choir	lp: decca (usa) DX 132
	saint hedwig's choir	cd: dg 439 6842
	radev	
	haefliger	
	borg	

ALESSANDRO SCARLATTI (1659-1725)

su le sponde del tebro, solo cantata
munich	*soprano soloist*	lp: dg LPEM 19 291/SLPEM 136 281
30 april-	**k.richter**	cd: dg 435 1422
1 may	munich bach	
1961	orchestra	

OTHMAR SCHOECK (1886-1957)

das bescheidene wünschlein (damals ganz zuerst am anfang)
munich	engel, piano	lp: dg LPEM 19 136
october		
1957		

mit einem gemalten bande (kleine blumen kleine blätter)
munich	engel, piano	lp: dg LPEM 19 136
october		
1957		

nachruf (du liebe treue laute)
munich	engel, piano	lp: dg LPEM 19 136
october		
1957		

reiselied (durch feld und buchenhallen)
munich	engel, piano	lp: dg LPEM 19 136
october		
1957		

FRANZ SCHUBERT (1797-1828)

mass in a flat
regensburg	*soprano soloist*	lp: dg 139 108
11-14	**ratzinger**	
july	bavarian radio	
1965	orchestra	
	regensburg	
	cathedral choir	
	höffgen	
	haefliger	
	uhde	

die forelle (in einem bächlein helle)
munich	engel, piano	lp: dg LPEM 19 136
october		
1957		

der hirt auf dem felsen (wenn auf dem höchsten fels ich steh')
munich	engel, piano	lp: dg LPEM 19 136
october	gall, clarinet	cd: dg 447 3342
1957		

du bist die ruh
munich	engel, piano	lp: dg LPEM 19 136
october		
1957		

la pastorella (es blüht auf blum'gen rasen)
munich	engel, piano	lp: dg LPEM 19 136
october		
1957		

seligkeit (freuden sonder zahl)
munich	engel, piano	lp: dg LPEM 19 136
october		
1957		

maria stader recorded a further group of schubert lieder for westminster, accompanied by jörg demus

ROBERT SCHUMANN (1810-1856)
maria stader recorded the song cycle frauenliebe und –leben for westminster, accompanied by jörg demus

GIUSEPPE VERDI (1813-1901)

messa da requiem

berlin	*soprano soloist*	lp: dg LPM 18 155-18 156/
22-26	**fricsay**	LPM 18 157-18 158
september	rso berlin	lp: decca (usa) DX 118
1953	rias choir	cd: dg 447 4422
	hedwig's	
	cathedral choir	
	radev	
	krebs	
	borg	

berlin	**fricsay**	lp: dg 2721 171
23 october	rso berlin	cd: dg 429 0762/439 6842
1960	hedwig's	*recorded at a public concert*
	cathedral choir	
	dominguez	
	carelli	
	sardi	

la traviata, excerpts (follie! sempre libera!; addio del passato)
harburg *role of violetta* lp: dg LPEM 19 139/SLPEM 136 005
15-17 **schmidt-** lp: dg heliodor 2548 117
february **isserstedt**
1958 ndr orchestra
sung in german

la traviata, excerpt (un di felice)
harburg *role of violetta* lp: dg LPEM 19 139/SLPEM 136 005
15-17 **schmidt-** lp: dg heliodor 2548 117
february **isserstedt**
1958 ndr orchestra
haefliger
sung in german

la traviata, excerpt (madamigella valéry?)
harburg *role of violetta* lp: dg LPEM 19 139/SLPEM 136 005
15-17 **schmidt-** lp: dg heliodor 2548 117
february **isserstedt**
1958 ndr orchestra
winters
sung in german

la traviata, excerpt (parigi o cara)
harburg *role of violetta* 45: dg EPL 30 606/SEPL 121 606
15-17 **schmidt-** lp: dg LPEM 19 139/SLPEM 136 005
february **isserstedt** lp: dg heliodor 2548 117
1958 ndr orchestra
haefliger
sung in german

la traviata, excerpt (prendi quest' e l'immagine)
harburg *role of violetta* lp: dg LPEM 19 139/SLPEM 136 005
15-17 **schmidt-** lp: dg heliodor 2548 117
february **isserstedt**
1958 ndr orchestra
haefliger
winters
sung in german

la traviata, excerpt (act 2 finale)
harburg	*role of violetta*	lp: dg LPEM 19 139/SLPEM 136 005
15-17	**schmidt-**	lp: dg heliodor 2548 117
february	**isserstedt**	
1958	ndr orchestra	
	and chorus	
	zollenkopf	
	haefliger	
	winters	
	sellentin	
	stuckmann	
	sung in german	

the excerpts from la traviata were recorded as part of a continuous querschnitt

ANTONIO VIVALDI (1675-1741)

gloria in d rv589, arranged by casella
florence	*soprano soloist*	lp: dg LPM 18 788/SLPM 138 788
24-25	**bartoletti**	
june	maggio musicale	
1962	orchestra	
	and chorus	
	rota	

MISCELLANEOUS

in dulci jubilo/european christmas carols: o du fröhliche; on christmas night; als die welt verloren; maria durch ein' dornwald ging; herbei o ihr gläubigen; es ist ein ros' entsprungen; marie et joseph; in dulci jubilo; kommet ihr hirten; vom himmel hoch; freu dich erd' und sternenzelt; o jesulein zart; d'ou viens-tu?; ach du mein liebes jesulein; seht das kindlein weinet; kindelein zart; schlaf mein kindlein; stille nacht

munich	**rothschuh**	lp: dg LPEM 19 266/SLPEM 136 266
28 May-	instrumental	*recordings completed on 25 june 1961*
1 june	ensemble	
1961	münchner	
	chorknaben	
	bilgram, organ	

elfride trötschel
1913-1958

JOHANN SEBASTIAN BACH (1685-1750)
elfride trötschel is soprano soloist in a radio broadcast of matthäus-passion conducted by fritz lehmann and issued by discophiles francais, allegro royale, vox, dante and music and arts

GEORGES BIZET (1838-1875)

carmen, excerpt (je dis que rien ne m'épouvante)
stuttgart   *role of micaela*   dg unpublished
14 july   **leitner**
1951   württembergisches
                staatsorchester
                sung in german

elfride trötschel also recorded the aria in dresden for mitteldeutscher rundfunk, published on the basf/acanta label

carmen, excerpt (parle-moi de ma mere)
stuttgart   *role of micaela*   78: dg LV 36 003
14 july   **leitner**   45: dg NL 32 203
1951   württembergisches
                staatsorchester
                w.ludwig
                sung in german

elfride trötschel also recorded the duet in dresden for mitteldeutscher rundfunk, published on the basf/acanta label
a 1942 complete recording of the opera conducted by karl böhm, in which trötschel takes the role of frasquita, is published by preiser and cantus classics

ANTONIN DVORAK (1841-1904)

the jacobin, excerpt (there is no hope)
stuttgart	*role of julie*	45: dg EPL 30 555
5-9	**leitner**	lp: dg LPM 18 057/LPEM 19 036
july	württem-	lp: dg heliodor 2548 061
1952	bergisches	lp: eterna 820 306
	staatsorchester	
	sung in german	

the jacobin, excerpt (we wandered in distant lands)
stuttgart	*role of julie*	45: dg EPL 30 555
5-9	**leitner**	lp: dg LPM 18 057/LPEM 19 036
july	württem-	lp: dg heliodor 2548 061
1952	staatsor	lp: eterna 820 306
	günter	
	sung in german	

a further excerpt from the jacobin was recorded for reichsrundfunk, conducted by karl elmendorff and published by preiser

rusalka, excerpt (o silver moon)
munich	*role of rusalka*	45: dg EPL 30 104
27 january	**heger**	lp: dg LPM 18 057/LPEM 19 036/
1951	munich	2548 061
	philharmonic	lp: eterna 820 306
	sung in german	

elfride trötschel took part in a complete recording of the opera for mitteldeutscher rundfunk in dresden, conducted by joseph keilberth and published on the american urania label

HERMANN GOETZ (1840-1876)

elfride trötschel sings the role of bianca in a reichsrundfunk recording of der widerspenstigen zähmung conducted by karl elmendorff and published by preiser and cantus classics

DIE JAHRESZEITEN

HAYDN

FRANZ JOSEF HAYDN (1732-1809)

die jahreszeiten
berlin
21-28
january
1952

soprano soloist
fricsay
rso berlin
rias choir
saint hedwig's
cathedral choir
w.ludwig
greindl

lp: dg LPM 18 025-18 028/
    LPM 18 486-18 488
lp: dg heliodor 2701 010
lp: decca (usa) DX 123
cd: dg 474 3832

FRANZ LEHAR (1870-1948)

die lustige witwe, querschnitt
munich
september
1951

role of hanna
nick
munich
philharmonic
and chorus
w.ludwig
w.hofmann

78: polydor LM 58 601
45: polydor EPH 20 040
lp: polydor LPH 45 020/LPHM 46 510
lp: decca (usa) DL 4001
lp: dg heliodor 478 107

RUGGIERO LEONCAVALLO (1858-1919)

i pagliacci, excerpt (stridono lassu)
stuttgart
31 march
1951

role of nedda   45: dg NL 32 133
leitner
württembergisches
staatsorchester
sung in german

ALBERT LORTZING (1801-1851)

der waffenschmied, excerpt (er schläft! wir alle sind in angst und not!)
stuttgart	*role of marie*	45: dg NL 32 133
5-9	**leitner**	lp: dg LPM 18 057/LPEM 19 036/
july	württem-	lp: dg heliodor 2548 061
1952	bergisches	lp: eterna 820 306
	staatsorchester	

GUSTAV MAHLER (1860-1911)

elfride trötschel is soprano soloist in two different performances of the fourth symphony, both conducted by otto klemperer, and published by movimento musica (wdr cologne) and melodram / arkadia (rso berlin) respectively

WOLFGANG AMADEUS MOZART (1756-1791)

don giovanni, excerpt (la ci darem la mano)
stuttgart	*role of zerlina*	78: dg LV 36 087
8 july	**leitner**	45: dg NL 32 016
1952	württem-	lp: dg LPE 17 014
	bergisches	
	staatsorchester	
	günter	
	sung in german	

don giovanni, excerpts (vedrai carino; batti batti)
stuttgart	*role of zerlina*	dg unpublished
12 october	**leitner**	
1951	württembergisches	
	staatsorchester	
	sung in german	

le nozze di figaro, excerpt (venite inginocchiatevi)

stuttgart	*role of susanna*	78: dg LVM 72 305
14 july	**leitner**	45: dg NL 32 025/EPL 30 512
1951	württem- bergisches staatsorchester	lp: dg LPM 18 558-18 559 lp: decca (usa) DL 4065

stuttgart	**leitner**	45: dg NL 32 216
14 july	württem-	lp: dg LPEM 19066
1951	bergisches staatsorchester *sung in german*	lp: dg heliodor 89 539

le nozze di figaro, excerpt (deh vieni non tardar)

stuttgart	*role of susanna*	78: dg LV 36 011
13 july	**leitner**	45: dg NL 32 025/EPL 30 512
1951	württem- bergisches staatsorchester	

stuttgart	**leitner**	45: dg NL 32 216
13 july	württem-	lp: dg LPEM 19 066
1951	bergisches staatsorchester *sung in german*	lp: dg heliodor 89 539

elfride trötschel also sings the role of ilia in an unpublished wdr cologne recording of idomeneo conducted by joseph keilberth

CLAUDIO MONTEVERDI (1567-1643)
elfride trötschel sings the role of euridice in a recording of l'orfeo conducted by helmut koch and published by discophiles francais, haydn society, eterna and vox

JACQUES OFFENBACH (1819-1880)
elfride trötschel sings the role of antonia in a wdr cologne performance of les contes d'hoffmann conducted by eugen szenkar and published by gebhardt

CARL ORFF (1895-1982)

carmina burana

munich	*soprano soloist*	lp: dg LP 16 045-16 046/LP 16 068-16 069/
5-10	**jochum**	LPM 18 303/LPM 18 483-18 485
october	bavarian radio	lp: decca (usa) DL 9706
1952	orchestra	cd: dg 445 0782/461 2192/474 1312
	and chorus	
	kuen	
	braun	
	hoppe	

elfride trötschel is also soprano soloist in an unpublished wdr cologne performance of trionfo di afrodite conducted by wolfgang sawallisch

HANS PFITZNER (1869-1949)

palestrina, excerpt (allein in dunkler tiefe)
berlin	*role of ighino*	78: dg LM 68 420
4 october	**heger**	45: dg NL 32 204
1949	komische oper orchestra members of komische oper and saint hedwig's choirs streich schlemm klose fehenberger	cd: preiser 89520

elfride trötschel is soprano soloist in an unpublished wdr cologne recording of the oratorio von deutscher seele conducted by joseph keilberth

GIACOMO PUCCINI (1858-1924)

la boheme, excerpt (sono andati)
berlin	*role of mimi*	78: dg LM 68 432
19 september	**schmitz**	45: dg NL 32 048
1949	komische oper orchestra fehenberger *sung in german*	

la boheme, excerpt (addio dolce svegliare alla mattina)
berlin	*role of mimi*	78: dg LM 68432
19 september	**schmitz**	45: dg NL 32 048
1949	komische oper orchestra streich fehenberger fischer-dieskau *sung in german*	cd: dg 463 5202/463 5002

BEDRICH SMETANA (1824-1884)

the bartered bride, excerpt (faithful love cannot be marred)
munich   *role of marenka*   78: dg LVM 72 062
27 january   **heger**   45: dg EPL 30 104
1951   munich
    philharmonic
    sung in german

the bartered bride, excerpt (alone at last! that dream of love!)
stuttgart   *role of marenka*   78: dg LVM 72 398
5 july   **leitner**
1952   württembergisches
    staatsorchester
    sung in german

JOHANN STRAUSS (1825-1899)

die fledermaus, querschnitt
cologne   *role of rosalinde*   78: polydor LM 58 612
1952   **marszalek**   45: polydor EPH 20 038
    wdr orchestra   lp: polydor LPH 45 025/LPHM 46 664
    and chorus   *excerpts*
    streich   lp: polydor LPHM 46 757/2430 243
    anders   cd: dg 447 6832
    w.hofmann
    schneider

der zigeunerbaron, querschnitt
cologne   *role of saffi*   78: polydor LM 58 613
1952   **marszalek**   45: polydor EPH 20 050
    wdr orchestra   lp: polydor LPH 45 025/LPHM 46 664
    and chorus   *excerpts*
    anders   lp: polydor LPHM 46 757/2430 243
    peter   lp: dg 2721 212
    kusche

RICHARD STRAUSS (1864-1949)

der rosenkavalier, excerpt (mir ist die ehre widerfahren)
stuttgart	*role of sophie*	78: dg LVM 72 139
12 july	**leitner**	lp: dg LPE 17 043
1951	württem-	
	bergisches	
	staatsorchester	
	milinkovic	

der rosenkavalier, excerpt (mein gott es war nicht mehr als eine farce!)
stuttgart	*role of sophie*	lp: dg LPM 18 011
9-11	**leitner**	lp: dg heliodor 89 698/479 012
october	württem-	lp: decca (usa) DL 9606
1951	bergisches	
	staatsorchester	
	lemnitz	
	milinkovic	

der rosenkavalier, excerpt (hab mir's gelobt/ist ein traum kann nicht wirklich sein)
stuttgart	*role of sophie*	78: dg LVM 72 121
9-11	**leitner**	45: dg EPL 30 141
october	württem-	lp: dg LPM 18 011
1951	bergisches	lp: dg heliodor 89 698/479 012
	staatsorchester	lp: decca (usa) DL 9606
	lemnitz	
	milinkovic	

PIOTR TCHAIKOVSKY (1840-1893)

evgeny onegin, excerpt (tatiana's letter scene)
munich	*role of tatiana*	lp: dg LPM 18 057/LPEM 19023/
26 january	**heger**	LPEM 19 036
1951	munich	lp: dg heliodor 2548 061
	philharmonic	lp: eterna 820 306
	sung in german	

GIUSEPPE VERDI (1813-1901)

elfride trötschel sings the role of laura in the opera luisa miller, recorded in dresden by the reichsrundfunk and conducted by karl elmendorff, and published by preiser. however, preiser incorrectly names the singer of laura as trude eipperle

elfride trötschel also sings the role of violetta in an unpublished berlin radio performance of act three of la traviata, and desdemona in the willow song and ave maria from otello, all conducted by ferenc fricsay

CARL MARIA VON WEBER (1786-1826)

elfride trötschel performs in two dresden recordings of der freischütz: in the role of ännchen conducted for the reichsrundfunk by karl elmendorff and published by preiser, and in the role of agathe conducted by rudolf kempe for mitteldeutscher rundfunk and published by urania, vox, basf/acanta, dante and arkadia

annelies
kupper
1906-1987

EUGEN D'ALBERT (1864-1932)

tiefland, excerpt (ich weiss nicht wer mein vater war)
munich	*role of marta*	78: dg LVM 72 378
7-19	**rother**	45: dg EPL 30 301
june	munich	lp: dg LPE 17 002
1953	philharmonic	lp: dg heliodor 89 661
	böhme	

tiefland, excerpt (sein bin ich!)
munich	*role of marta*	lp: dg LPE 17 002
7-19	**rother**	lp: dg heliodor 89 661
june	munich	
1953	philharmonic	

die toten augen, excerpt (psyche wandelt durch säulenhallen)
munich	*role of myrtocle*	45: dg NL 32 014/EPL 30 472
15 december	**reinshagen**	
1953	bamberg	
	symphony	

JOHANN SEBASTIAN BACH (1685-1750)

annelies kupper is soprano soloist in cantata no 208 "was mir behagt ist die munt're jagd" recorded for electrola and conducted by karl forster

LUDWIG VAN BEETHOVEN (1770-1827)

annelies kupper is soprano soloist in a wdr cologne performance of missa solemnis, issued by movimento musica/frequenz and conducted by otto klemperer

ALBAN BERG (1885-1935)

annelies kupper is soprano soloist in two unpublished wdr cologne performances of the lulu suite, conducted by hans rosbaud and nino sanzogno respectively; in an unpublished wdr cologne performance of the wozzeck fragments conducted by ferenc fricsay; and in two further performances of the wozzeck fragments conducted by erich kleiber, published by cetra and stradivarius respectively

ALEXANDER BORODIN (1833-1887)
annelies kupper sings the role of jaroslavna in an unpublished wdr performance of prince igor conducted by ljubomir romansky

BENJAMIN BRITTEN (1913-1976)
annelies kupper sings the role of female chorus in an unpublished radio broadcast of the rape of lucretia conducted by josef krips

ANTON BRUCKNER (1824-1896)
annelies kupper sings the soprano part in a bavarian radio performance of the te deum conducted by eugen jochum and published by orfeo

UMBERTO GIORDANO (1867-1948)
annelies kupper sings in an excerpt from andrea chenier recorded by bavarian radio, conducted by kurt eichhorn and published by preiser

EDVARD GRIEG (1843-1907)

last spring
munich	**rieger**	lp: dg LPEM 19 059
9-10	munich	
november	philharmonic	
1955	*sung in german*	

solveig's song/peer gynt
munich	**rieger**	45: dg NL 32 120
9-10	munich	lp: dg LPEM 19 059
november	philharmonic	lp: polydor LPHM 48 692
1955	*sung in german*	

solveig's cradle song/peer gynt
munich	**rieger**	45: dg NL 32 120
9-10	munich	lp: dg LPEM 19 059
november	philharmonic	
1955	*sung in german*	

a swan
munich	**rieger**	lp: dg LPEM 19 059
9-10	munich	
november	philharmonic	
1955	*sung in german*	

KARL AMADEUS HARTMANN (1905-1963)

lamento, cantata after three poems by andreas gryphius
hannover   seemann, piano   lp: dg LP 16 135
9-11   *work commissioned by the deutsche grammophon*
december   *gesellschaft*
1956

FRANZ JOSEF HAYDN (1732-1809)

annelies kupper is soprano soloist in an unpublished wdr cologne performance of die schöpfung conducted by joseph keilberth

PAUL HINDEMITH (1895-1963)

annelies kupper performs the song-cycle das marienleben in its 1949 version on the christophorus label

ARTHUR HONEGGER (1892-1955)

annelies kupper sings the role of virgin mary in an unpublished wdr cologne performance of jeanne d'arc au bucher, conducted by paul sacher

GISELHER KLEBE (born 1925)

annelies kupper is soprano soloist in an unpublished wdr performance of raskolnikows traum (dramatic scena for soprano, clarinet and orchestra) conducted by nino sanzogno

ERICH WOLFGANG KORNGOLD (1897-1957)

die tote stadt, excerpt (glück das mir verblieb)
munich   *role of marietta*   45: dg NL 32 014/EPL 30 472
15 december   **reinshagen**   lp: dg LPEM 19 015
1953   bamberg
                   symphony
                   fehenberger

GUSTAV MAHLER (1860-1911)
annelies kupper is soprano soloist in symphony no 4 conducted by bruno walter and published by the japanese label green hill; and takes the part of first soprano and magna peccatrix in symphony no 8 conducted by eduard flipse, published by philips

WOLFGANG AMADEUS MOZART (1756-1791)

le nozze di figaro, excerpt (porgi amor)
stuttgart	*role of contessa*	45: dg EPL 30 483
8 may	**leitner**	lp: decca (usa) DL 4065
1952	württem-	
	bergisches	
	staatsorchester	

stuttgart	**leitner**	78: dg LV 36 087
8 may	württem-	45: dg NL 32 016
1952	bergisches	lp: dg LPEM 19 066
	staatsorchester	lp: dg heliodor 89 539
	sung in german	

le nozze di figaro, excerpt (dove sono)
stuttgart	*role of contessa*	45: dg EPL 30 483
8 may	**leitner**	lp: dg LPM 18 558-18 559
1952	württem-	lp: dg heliodor 478 124
	bergisches	lp: decca (usa) DL 4065
	staatsorchester	

stuttgart	**leitner**	78: dg LVM 72 305
8 may	württem-	lp: dg LPEM 19 066
1952	bergisches	lp: dg heliodor 89 539
	staatsorchester	
	sung in german	

le nozze di figaro, excerpt (che soave zeffiretto)
munich *role of contessa* 45: dg EPL 30 274
27 february **sandberg** lp: preiser PR 135014
1954 munich
 philharmonic
 schlemm
 sung in german

don giovanni, excerpt (or sai chi l'onore)
munich *role of anna* 45: dg EPL 30 006
12 december **heger** lp: dg LPE 17 014
1950 munich
 philharmonic
 sung in german

don giovanni, excerpt (crudele? non mi dir)
munich *role of anna* 45: dg EPL 30 006
12 december **heger**
1950 munich
 philharmonic
 sung in german

annelies kupper sings the role of first lady in a wdr cologne performance of die zauberflöte conducted by joseph keilberth and published by myto

CARL ORFF (1895-1982)

catulli carmina, ludi scaenici
munich	*soprano soloist*	lp: dg LPM 18 293/LPM 18 304/
2 june	**jochum**	LPM 18 483-18 485
1954	bavarian radio	lp: decca (usa) DL 9824
	orchestra	cd: dg 474 1312
	and chorus	*excerpts*
	holm	lp: dg LP 16 117/LPE 17 021
		recording completed on 13 november 1955

trionfo di afrodite, concerto scenico
munich	*soprano soloist*	lp: dg LPM 18 305/LPM 18 483-18 485
12 july	**jochum**	lp: decca (usa) DL 9824
1955	bavarian radio	cd: dg 474 1312
	orchestra	*recording completed on 8 october 1955*
	and chorus	
	lindermeier	
	wiese-lange	
	holm	
	delorko	
	böhme	

FRANZ SCHUBERT (1797-1828)

am see (sitz' ich im gras am glatten see)
harburg   altmann, piano   45: dg EPL 30 304
29 april
1952

an den mond (füllest wieder busch und tal)
harburg   altmann, piano   45: dg EPL 30 304
29 april
1952

blanka (wenn mich einsam lüfte fächeln)
harburg   altmann, piano   45: dg EPL 30 304
29 april
1952

geheimnis (sag an wer lehrt dich lieder)
harburg   altmann, piano   45: dg EPL 30 304
29 april
1952

nachtviolen dunkle augen
harburg   altmann, piano   45: dg EPL 30 304
29 april
1952

seligkeit (freuden sonder zahl)
harburg   altmann, piano   45: dg EPL 30 304
29 april
1952

ROBERT SCHUMANN (1810-1856)

geisternähe (was weht um meine schläfe?)
harburg   altmann, piano   45: dg EPL 30 289
29 april
1952

jasminenstrauch (grün ist der jasminenstrauch)
harburg   altmann, piano   45: dg EPL 30 289
29 april
1952

meine rose (dem holden lenzgeschmeide)
harburg   altmann, piano   45: dg EPL 30 289
29 april
1952

o ihr herren o ihr werten
harburg   altmann, piano   45: dg EPL 30 289
29 april
1952

schneeglöckchen (der schnee der gestern noch in flöckchen)
harburg   altmann, piano   45: dg EPL 30 289
29 april
1952

stille tränen (du bist vom schlaf erstanden)
harburg   altmann, piano   45: dg EPL 30 289
29 april
1952

RICHARD STRAUSS (1864-1949)

ariadne auf naxos, excerpt (es gibt ein reich)
stuttgart	*role of ariadne*	45: dg EPL 30 119
6 may	**leitner**	
1952	württem- bergisches staatsorchester	

daphne, excerpt (o bleib geliebter tag)
munich	*role of daphne*	lp: dg LPM 18 090
27 august	**lehmann**	cd: preiser 90487
1951	munich philharmonic	

daphne, excerpt (ich komm' grünende bäume)
munich	*role of daphne*	lp: dg LPM 18 090
27 august	**lehmann**	cd: preiser 90487
1951	munich philharmonic	

annelies kupper sings the title role in the belated world premiere performance of die liebe der danae conducted by clemens krauss and published by discocorp, melodram and orfeo; and the role of aithra in a munich festival performance of die ägyptische helena conducted by joseph keilberth and published by melodram and orfeo

annelies kupper sings the role of chrysothemis in a reichsrundfunk recording of elektra conducted by eugen jochum and published by acanta and arkadia, and in a hessischer rundfunk performance conducted by kurt schröder published by melodram

die georgine (warum so spät erst?)
harburg altmann, piano 45: dg EPL 30 297
30 april
1952

meinem kinde (du schläfst und sachte neig' ich mich)
harburg altmann, piano 45: dg EPL 30 297
30 april
1952

die nacht (aus dem walde tritt die nacht)
harburg altmann, piano 45: dg EPL 30 297
30 april
1952

schön sind doch kalt die himmelssterne
harburg altmann, piano 45: dg EPL 30 297
30 april
1952

die verschwiegenen (ich habe wohl es sei hier laut)
harburg altmann, piano 45: dg EPL 30 297
30 april
1952

die zeitlose (auf frisch gemähtem weideplatz)
harburg altmann, piano 45: dg EPL 30 297
30 april
1952

GIUSEPPE VERDI (1813-1901)

aida, excerpt (fu la sorte dell' armi)
stuttgart   *role of aida*   lp: dg LPM 18 009/LPEM 19 027
2 april   **leitner**
1951   württem-
bergisches
staatsorchester
and chorus
höngen
sung in german

aida, excerpt (ciel mio padre!/rivedrai la foreste imbalsamate)
munich   *role of aida*   lp: dg LPM 18 009/LPEM 19 027
may   **solti**
1949   bavarian state
orchestra
reinmar
sung in german

aida, excerpt (pur ti riveggo)
munich   *role of aida*   lp: dg LPM 18 009/LPEM 19 027
may   **solti**
1949   bavarian state
orchestra
fehenberger
sung in german

annelies kupper sings the role of aida in a hessischer rundfunk performance of the opera conducted by kurt schröder and published by myto

la forza del destino, excerpt (son giunta!/madre pietosa vergine/infelice delusa rejetta!)
stuttgart   *role of leonora*   78: dg LVM 72 225-72 226
7-8   **leitner**   lp: dg LP 16 020/LPE 17 030
may   württem-
1952   bergisches
staatsorchester
and chorus
greindl
neidlinger
sung in german

annelies kupper sings the role of alice ford in a complete unpublished stuttgart radio broadcast of falstaff conducted by hans müller-kray, and the role of desdemona in two complete unpublished bavarian radio broadcasts of otello conducted by eugen jochum and ferenc fricsay respectively

RICHARD WAGNER (1813-1883)

der fliegende holländer

berlin	*role of senta*	lp: dg LPM 18 063-18 065/
october	**fricsay**	LPM 18 116-18 118/2701 009
1952	rso berlin	lp: decca (usa) DX 124
	rias choir	cd: dg 439 7142
	wagner	*excerpts*
	windgassen	45: dg EPL 30 024/EPL 30 124
	haefliger	lp: dg LPEM 19 122
	metternich	
	greindl	

lohengrin

munich	*role of elsa*	lp: dg LPM 18 084-18 088/
15-22	**jochum**	LPM 18 119-18 123/2703 001
december	bavarian radio	lp: decca (usa) DX 131
1952	orchestra	*excerpts*
	and chorus	45: dg EPL 30 048
	braun	lp: dg LPEM 19 107
	fehenberger	lp: dg heliodor 89 654
	frantz	
	von rohr	

die meistersinger von nürnberg, excerpt (selig wie die sonne)

munich	*role of eva*	45: dg EPL 30 112
15 may	**leitner**	lp: dg LPEM 19 047
1955	munich	lp: dg heliodor 478 126
	philharmonic	lp: decca (usa) DL 9895
	töpper	
	windgassen	
	holm	
	herrmann	

annelies kupper sings the part of eva in a bayerische staatsoper performance conducted by eugen jochum and published by melodram and myto
annelies kupper also sings the part of eva in an excerpt from an ndr broadcast conducted by hans schmidt-isserstedt and published by preiser

tannhäuser, excerpt (o fürstin!)
berlin   *role of elisabeth*   lp: dg LPEM 19 106
5 december   **kraus**   lp: dg heliodor 2548 156
1956   rso berlin
            windgassen

wolfgang windgassen
1914-1974

EUGEN D'ALBERT (1864-1932)

tiefland, excerpt (ich grüss' noch einmal die berge)
munich	*role of pedro*	78: dg LVM 72 378
7-19	**rother**	45: dg EPL 30 301
june	munich	lp: dg LPE 17 002
1953	philharmonic	lp: dg heliodor 89 661

tiefland, excerpt (schau her das ist ein taler!)
munich	*role of pedro*	78: dg LVM 72 378
7-19	**rother**	45: dg EPL 30 301
june	munich	lp: dg LPE 17 002
1953	philharmonic	lp: dg heliodor 89 661

wolfgang windgassen also sings this aria in a stuttgart radio performance conducted by bertil wetzelsberger and published by myto and uracant

wolfgang windgassen sings the role of aurelius galba in die toten augen, in a stuttgart radio performance conducted by walter born and published by myto

LUDWIG VAN BEETHOVEN (1770-1827)

wolfgang windgassen sings the role of florestan in fidelio in performances conducted by wilhelm furtwängler published by emi/electrola (studio) and various labels (live); excerpts from a live performance in stuttgart conducted by ferdinand leitner are issued by uracant; and in a further complete performance of the opera conducted by herbert von karajan and issued privately in vienna

wolfgang windgassen is also tenor soloist in a bayreuth festival performance of the beethoven ninth conducted by wilhelm furtwängler and published in japan by disques refrain

ALBERT LORTZING (1801-1851)

der wildschütz, excerpt (ich habe numero eins!)
stuttgart	*role of baron*	78: dg LM 73 043
4-6	**leitner**	45: dg EPL 30 123
september	württem-	lp: dg LPEM 19 009
1950	bergisches	lp: dg heliodor 89 649
	staatsorchester	
	wissmann	
	r.fischer	
	czubok	
	hann	

HANS PFITZNER (1869-1949)
wolfgang windgassen sings the role of siegnot in an excerpt from a stuttgart radio performance of die rose vom liebesgarten conducted by alfons rischner and published by myto and uracant

JOHANN STRAUSS (1825-1899)
wolfgang windgassen sings the role of orlofsky in a decca recording of die fledermaus conducted by karl böhm (also published in video format)

RICHARD STRAUSS (1864-1949)

salome, excerpt (du wolltest mich nicht deinen mund küssen lassen)

stuttgart	*role of herod*	lp: dg LPM 18 090
8-9	**leitner**	lp: decca (usa) DL 9778
april	württem-	
1951	bergisches	
	staatsorchester	
	goltz	
	plümacher	

wolfgang windgassen sings the role of aegisth in a performance of elektra conducted by karl böhm and published by historical recording enterprises and legato

wolfgang windgassen sings the title role in a stuttgart radio broadcast of excerpts from guntram conducted by alfons rischner and published by uracant

GIUSEPPE VERDI (1813-1901)
wolfgang windgassen sings the role of otello in a stuttgart television recording conducted by argeo quadri and published in the usa by lyric distribution

RICHARD WAGNER (1813-1883)

der fliegende holländer
berlin	*role of erik*	lp: dg LPM 18 063-18 065/
october	**fricsay**	LPM 18 116-18 118
1952	rso berlin	lp: dg heliodor 2701 009
	rias choir	cd: dg 439 7142
	kupper	*excerpts*
	wagner	45: dg EPL 30 024
	haefliger	lp: dg LPEM 19 122
	metternich	lp: dg heliodor 89 652
	greindl	

wolfgang windgassen also sings the role of erik in bayreuth festival performances of the opera conducted by hans knappertsbusch and published by discocorp and melodram

götterdämmerung, excerpt (zu neuen taten)
munich	*role of siegfried*	lp: dg LPEM 19 063
7-8	**ludwig**	lp: dg heliodor 89 800
september	bavarian radio	cd: dg 423 7202/474 4102
1955	orchestra	
	varnay	

götterdämmerung, excerpt (brünnhilde heilige braut!)
munich	*role of siegfried*	78: dg LV 36 083
26 june	**ludwig**	45: dg NL 32 144
1953	munich	lp: dg LPEM 19 106
	philharmonic	lp: dg heliodor 2548 156

wolfgang windgassen sings the complete role of siegfried in götterdämmerung in bayreuth festival performances conducted by clemens krauss, joseph keilberth and hans knappertsbusch published by melodram, conducted by georg solti published by decca and conducted by karl böhm published by philips

lohengrin, excerpt (in fernem land)
berlin *role of lohengrin* 45: dg EPL 30 261
5 december **kraus** lp: dg LPEM 19 106
1956 rso berlin lp: dg heliodor 2548 156

lohengrin, excerpt (mein lieber schwan)
berlin *role of lohengrin* 45: dg EPL 30 261
5 december **kraus** lp: dg LPEM 19 106
1956 rso berlin lp: dg heliodor 2548 156
wolfgang windgassen also sings this excerpt in a stuttgart radio broadcasr conducted by alfons rischner and published by uracant
wolfgang windgassen sings the complete role of lohengrin in bayreuth festival performances conducted by joseph keilberth (decca/teldec), eugen jochum (cetra and arkadia) and lorin maazel (melodram)

die meistersinger von nürnberg, excerpt (am stillen herd)
munich *role of stolzing* 45: dg NL 32 114
22 february **leitner** lp: dg LPEM 19 047
1955 munich lp: dg heliodor 478 126
 philharmonic lp: decca (usa) DL 9895
wolfgang windgassen also sings this excerpt in a stuttgart radio broadcast conducted by alfons rischner and published by uracant

die meistersinger von nürnberg, excerpt (morgenlich leuchtend)
munich *role of stolzing* 45: dg NL 32 114
22 february **leitner** lp: dg LPEM 19 047/2721 115
1955 munich lp: dg heliodor 478 126
 philharmonic lp: decca (usa) DL 9895
wolfgang windgassen also sings this excerpt in a stuttgart radio broadcast conducted by alfons rischner and published by uracant

die meistersinger von nürnberg, excerpt (selig wie die sonne)
munich	*role of stolzing*	45: dg EPL 30 112
15 may	**leitner**	lp: dg LPEM 19 047
1955	munich	lp: dg heliodor 478 126
	philharmonic	lp: decca (usa) DL 9895
	kupper	
	töpper	
	holm	
	herrmann	

wolfgang windgassen sings the complete role of stolzing in bayreuth festival performances conducted by andré cluytens (music and arts), hans knappertsbusch (melodram) and josef krips (unpublished)

parsifal, excerpt (nur eine waffe taugt)
berlin	*role of parsifal*	45: dg EPL 30 465
5 december	**kraus**	lp: dg LPEM 19 106
1956	rso berlin	lp: dg heliodor 2548 156

wolfgang windgassen sings the complete role of parsifal in a bayreuth festival performance conducted by hans knappertsbusch and published by decca, teldec and naxos; and in a rai roma performance conducted by eugen jochum and published by living stage

das rheingold
wolfgang windgassen sings the role of froh in 1952 bayreuth festival performance conducted by joseph keilberth and published by paragon; he is also listed in that role in the 1951 performances conducted by herbert von karajan and hans knappertsbusch but in the karajan performance issued by melodram windgassen is audibly not the singer of this role

rienzi, excerpt (allmächt'ger vater blick herab!)
munich	*role of rienzi*	45: dg EPL 30 226
10 february	**leitner**	lp: dg LPEM 19 106
1956	bamberg so	lp: dg heliodor 2548 156

wolfgang windgassen sings the role of rienzi in a stuttgart staatstheater performance conducted by lovro von matacic and published by living stage

siegfried, excerpt (notung neidliches schwert!/schmiede mein hammer!)
munich	*role of siegfried*	45: dg NL 32 220
10-11	**leitner**	lp: dg LPEM 19 106
february	bamberg so	lp: dg heliodor 2548 156
1956	carnuth	

siegfried, excerpt (dass der mein vater nicht ist)
munich	*role of siegfried*	lp: dg LPE 17 059
18 may	**leitner**	cd: dg 457 0212/457 0232
1955	munich philharmonic	

siegfried, excerpt (heil dir sonne!)
munich	*role of siegfried*	lp: dg LPEM 19 045/2721 115
june	**weigert**	lp: dg heliodor 478 127
1954	bavarian radio orchestra	cd: dg 423 7202/474 4102
	varnay	*2721 115 and 423 7202 begin only at ewig war ich*

wolfgang windgassen also sings the closing scene from siegfried in a stuttgart radio broadcast conducted by alfons rischner and published by myto

wolfgang windgassen sings the complete role of siegfried in bayreuth festival performances conducted by clemens krauss, joseph keilberth and hans knappertsbusch and in recordings conducted by georg solti for decca and karl böhm for philips

tannhäuser
berlin	*role of tannhäuser*	lp: dg 139 284-139 287/2711 008/ 2740 142
december	**gerdes**	cd: dg 471 7082
1968	deutsche oper orchestra and chorus	*excerpts*
	nilsson	lp: dg 2537 016
	laubenthal fischer-dieskau adam	*recording completed in february and may 1969*

tannhäuser, excerpt (inbrunst im herzen)
munich	*role of tannhäuser*	78: dg LV 36 101
19 june	**rother**	45: dg EPL 30 101
1953	munich philharmonic	lp: dg LPE 17 059/LPM 19 069

tannhäuser, excerpt (o fürstin!)
berlin	*role of tannhäuser*	lp: dg LPEM 19 106
5 december	**kraus**	lp: dg heliodor 2548 156
1956	rso berlin kupper	

wolfgang windgassen also sings this extract in a stuttgart radio performance conducted by alfons rischner and published by uracant

wolfgang windgassen also sings the complete role of tannhäuser in bayreuth festival performances conducted by andré cluytens, wolfgang sawallisch and otmar suitner, and the scene dir soll mein lied ertönen in a stuttgart radio broadcast conducted by alfons rischner and published by uracant

tristan und isolde
bayreuth	*role of tristan*	lp: dg KL 512-516/SKL 912-916/
july-	**böhm**	LPEM 19 221-19 225/
august	bayreuth	SLPEM 139 221-139 225/2713 001/
1966	festival	2740 144/415 3951
	orchestra	lp: philips 6747 243
	and chorus	cd: dg 415 3952/419 8892/449 7722
	nilsson	cd: philips 434 4202/434 4252
	ludwig	*excerpts*
	wächter	lp: dg 136 443/2537 001
	talvela	cd: dg 439 4692

tristan und isolde, sequence from act 2: isolde! tristan! geliebter!/o sink hernieder (love duet I)/einsam wachend/love duet II
bamberg	*role of tristan*	lp: dg LPEM 19 193/SLPEM 136 030
14-16	**leitner**	cd: dg 474 4102
april	bamberg so	*o sink hernieder and einsam wachend only*
1959	varnay	cd: dg 423 9552
	töpper	*o sink hernieder only*
		lp: dg 2538 058

wolfgang windgassen also recorded the love duet with martha mödl for telefunken, conducted by artur rother

tristan und isolde, excerpt (wie sie selig hehr und milde)
munich	*role of tristan*	45: dg EPL 30 025
26 june	**ludwig**	lp: dg LPEM 19 018/LPEM 19 106
1953	munich	lp: dg heliodor 2548 156
	philharmonic	

wolfgang windgassen sings the complete role of tristan in additional bayreuth festival performances conducted by wolfgang sawallisch and karl böhm and both published by melodram, in a florence performance conducted by artur rodzinski and published by cetra and in a japanese television performance conducted by pierre boulez and published by bel canto society

die walküre, act one
stuttgart	*role of siegmund*	lp: dg LPM 18 022-18 023
17-20	**leitner**	lp: dg heliodor 2548 735
november	württem-	lp: decca (usa) DX 121
1951	bergisches	cd: dg eloquence awaiting publication
	staatsorchester	*excerpts*
	müller	45: dg NL 32 144/EPL 30 031
	greindl	

die walküre, excerpt (siegmund sieh auf mich!)
munich	*role of siegmund*	lp: dg LPEM 19 063
6-7	**ludwig**	lp: dg heliodor 89 800
september	bavarian radio	cd: dg 423 7202/474 4102
1955	orchestra	
	varnay	

wolfgang windgassen sings the role of siegmund in a rai roma broadcast conducted by wilhelm furtwängler (published by mrf, arkadia and emi) and in bayreuth festival performances conducted by hans knappertsbusch (published by melodram and music and arts) and rudolf kempe (published by melodram)

CARL MARIA VON WEBER (1786-1826)

der freischütz, excerpt (durch die wälder)
munich	*role of max*	78: dg LVM 72 419
19 june	**rother**	45: dg EPL 30 226
1953	munich	lp: dg LPEM 19 013
	philharmonic	lp: dg heliodor 89 537
		lp: decca (usa) DL 9797
		lp: heliodor (usa) H 25016/HS 25016

ernst haefliger
born 1919

ADOLPHE ADAM (1803-1856)

le postillon de lonjumeau, excerpt (mes amis écoutez l'histoire!)
berlin   *role of chapelon*   45: dg EPL 30 591
29-30   **märzendorfer**
may   rso berlin
1961   *sung in german*

CARL PHILIPP EMANUEL BACH (1714-1788)

magnificat in d
harburg   *tenor soloist*   lp: dg archiv 198 367
13-17   **detel**
november   ndr orchestra
1965   städtischer chor
    stolte
    töpper
    mcdaniel

ernst haefliger also took part in a recording of the oratorio die israeliten in der wüste

JOHANN SEBASTIAN BACH (1685-1750)

cantata no 1 "wie schön leuchtet der morgenstern"
munich   *tenor soloist*   lp: dg archiv 198 465/2547 064/
july   **k.richter**   2722 022/2722 028
1968   munich bach   cd: dg 439 3682/439 3742
    orchestra
    and chorus
    mathis
    fischer-dieskau

cantata no 6 "sie werden aus saba alle kommen"
munich   *tenor soloist*   lp: dg archiv 2722 005
february   **k.richter**   cd: dg 439 3682/439 3692
1967   munich bach
    orchestra
    and chorus
    adam

cantata no 8 "liebster gott wann werd' ich sterben?"
ansbach	*tenor soloist*	lp: dg archiv APM 14 143/SAPM 198 028
july-	**k.richter**	cd: dg 439 3682/439 3872
august	munich bach	
1959	orchestra	
	and chorus	
	buckel	
	töpper	
	engen	

cantata no 21 "ich hatte viel bekümmernis"
munich	*tenor soloist*	lp: dg archiv 2533 049
july	**k.richter**	cd: dg 439 3682/439 3802
1969	munich bach	
	orchestra	
	and chorus	
	mathis	
	fischer-dieskau	

cantata no 26 "ach wie flüchtig ach wie nichtig!"
munich	*tenor soloist*	lp: dg archiv 198 402
october	**k.richter**	cd: dg 439 3682/439 3942
1966	munich bach	
	orchestra	
	and chorus	
	buckel	
	töpper	
	adam	

cantata no 45 "es ist dir gesagt mensch was gut ist"
ansbach	*tenor soloist*	lp: dg archiv APM 14 143/SAPM 198 028
july-	**k.richter**	cd: dg 439 3682/439 3872
august	munich bach	*excerpts*
1959	orchestra	lp: dg LPEM 19 268/SLPEM 136 268
	and chorus	
	töpper	
	engen	

cantata no 55 "ich armer mensch ich sündenknecht"
munich   *tenor soloist*   lp: dg archiv AP 13 072/SAP 195 004
february-   **k.richter**   cd: dg 439 3682/439 3942
march   munich bach
1959   orchestra
                 and chorus

cantata no 60 "o ewigkeit du donnerwort!"
munich   *tenor soloist*   lp: dg archiv APM 14 331/SAPM 198 331
february   **k.richter**   cd: dg 439 3682/439 3942
1964   munich bach
                 orchestra
                 and chorus
                 töpper
                 engen

cantata no 106 "gottes zeit ist die allerbeste zeit"
munich   *tenor soloist*   lp: dg archiv 198 402
october   **k.richter**   cd: dg 439 3682/439 3942
1966   munich bach
                 orchestra
                 and chorus
                 töpper
                 adam

cantata no 108 "es ist euch gut dass ich hingehe"
munich   *tenor soloist*   lp: dg archiv 2722 022
february   **k.richter**   cd: dg 439 3682/439 3742
1967   munich bach
                 orchestra
                 and chorus
                 töpper
                 adam

Bach · Kantaten · Cantatas
VOL. 3
HIMMELFAHRT · PFINGSTEN · TRINITATIS
Ascension Day · Whitsun · Trinity
Ascension · Pentecôte · Trinité

ARCHIV PRODUKTION

cantata no 124 "meinen jesum lass' ich nicht"
munich	*tenor soloist*	lp: dg archiv 2722 005
march	**k.richter**	cd: dg 439 3682/439 3692
1967	munich bach	
	orchestra	
	and chorus	
	schädle	
	töpper	
	adam	

cantata no 189 "meine seele rühmt und preist"
munich	*tenor soloist*	lp: dg archiv AP 13 072/SAP 195 004
february-	**k.richter**	*excerpts*
march	munich bach	lp: dg LPEM 19 268/SLPEM 136 268/
1959	orchestra	2535 745
	and chorus	

johannes-passion
leipzig	*evangelist and*	lp: dg archiv APM 14 036-14 038/
18-23	*tenor soloist*	APM 14 136-14 138
october	**k.richter**	cd: berlin classics BC 20152
1954	gewandhaus-	*excerpts*
	orchester	45: dg archiv EPA 37 081
	thomanerchor	*also issued on lp by eterna*
	giebel	
	höffgen	
	kelch	
	hudermann	

munich	**k.richter**	lp: dg archiv APM 14 328-14 330/
february-	munich bach	SAPM 198 328-198 330/2710 002
march	orchestra	2723 064/413 9441
1964	and chorus	cd: dg 413 6222/453 0072/463 7012
	lear	*excerpts*
	töpper	lp: dg LPEM 19 260/SLPEM 136 260/
	prey	2535 152/2535 626
	engen	

ernst haefliger also sings part of evangelist in a philips recording of johannes-passion conducted by eugen jochum

magnificat

munich	*tenor soloist*	lp: dg archiv AP 13 078/APM 14 197/
april	**k.richter**	SAP 195 078/SAPM 198 197/2722 018
1961	munich bach	cd: dg 419 4662/463 7012
	orchestra	*excerpts*
	and chorus	lp: dg LPEM 19 268/SLPEM 136 268/
	stader	2535 745
	töpper	
	fischer-dieskau	

ernst haefliger also recorded this part for nixa conducted by walter reinhart, subsequently issued by concert hall and musical masterpiece society

mass in b minor

munich	*tenor soloist*	lp: dg archiv APM 14 190-14 192/
february-	**k.richter**	SAPM 198 190-198 192/2710 001/
april	munich bach	2722 017/2723 065
1961	orchestra	cd: dg 427 1552
	and chorus	*excerpts*
	stader	lp: dg LPEM 19 268/SLPEM 136 268/
	töpper	LPEM 19 300/SLPEM 136 300/
	engen	2533 313/2535 745
tokyo	**k.richter**	cd: dg 463 7012
9 may	munich bach	*recorded at a public concert*
1969	orchestra	
	and chorus	
	buckel	
	höffgen	
	schramm	

ernst haefliger also recorded this part for eterna conducted by rudolf mauersberger and for philips conducted by lorin maazel

matthäus-passion

munich	*evangelist and*	lp: dg archiv APM 14 125-14 128/
june-	*tenor soloist*	SAPM 198 009-198 012/2722 010
august	**k.richter**	cd: dg 439 3382/463 7012
1958	munich bach	*excerpts*
	orchestra	45: dg archiv EPA 37 189/EPA 37 190/
	and chorus	EPA 37 191
	seefried	lp: dg LPEM 19 233/SLPEM 136 233/
	töpper	LPEM 19 268/SLPEM 136 268/
	engen	2535 220
	fischer-dieskau	

ernst haefliger also recorded these parts for philips conducted by eugen jochum and for vanguard conducted by johannes somary; also on an unidentified label conducted by pablo casals and sung in english

ernst haefliger also recorded the tenor part in osteroratorium for philips conducted by lorin maazel

LUDWIG VAN BEETHOVEN (1770-1827)
fidelio

munich	*role of florestan*	lp: dg LPM 18 390-18 391/
may	**fricsay**	SLPM 138 390-138 391/2726 088/
1957	bavarian state	2727 006
	orchestra	cd: dg 437 3452/453 1062
	and chorus	*excerpts*
	rysanek	45: dg EPL 30 406
	seefried	lp: dg LPEM 19 215/SLPEM 136 215/
	lenz	135 127/2535 745/2535 298
	frick	cd: dg 437 6772
	engen	*recording completed in september 1957*
	fischer-dieskau	

symphony no 9 "choral"

berlin	*tenor soloist*	lp: dg LPM 18 512-18 513/
28 december	**fricsay**	SLPM 138 002-138 003/2535 203/
1957-	rso berlin	2730 015
2 january	saint hedwig's	lp: dg heliodor 89 727-89 728/2700 108
1958	choir	cd: dg 445 4002/445 4012
	seefried	
	forrester	
	fischer-dieskau	

ernst haefliger also sings this part in a studio recording for columbia conducted by herbert von karajan, and in live recordings conducted by wilhelm furtwängler and herbert von karajan; and in an unpublished wdr cologne recording conducted by joseph keilberth

ernst haefliger sings the tenor part in missa solemnis conducted by george szell and issued privately

an die ferne geliebte, song cycle: auf dem hügel sitz' ich spähend; wo die berge so blau; leichte segler in den höhen; diese wolken in den höhen; es kehret der maien; nimm sie hin denn diese lieder

berlin	werba, piano	lp: dg LPM 18 843/SLPM 138 843
5-12		
october		
1962		

BORIS BLACHER (1903-1975)

13 ways of looking at a blackbird, song cycle on words by wallace stevens

berlin	*tenor soloist*	lp: dg LPM 18 759/SLPM 138 759
8 june	drolc string	
1961	quartet	

JOHANNES BRAHMS (1833-1897)

botschaft (wehe lüftchen lind und lieblich)
berlin   klust, piano   lp: dg LPEM 19 096
10-12
november
1956

eine gute gute nacht
berlin   klust, piano   lp: dg LPEM 19 096
10-12
november
1956

geheimnis (o frühlingsabenddämmerung)
berlin   klust, piano   45: dg EPL 30 316
10-12   lp: dg LPEM 19 096
november
1956

in waldeinsamkeit (ich sass zu deinen füssen)
berlin   klust, piano   45: dg EPL 30 316
10-12   lp: dg LPEM 19 096
november
1956

meine liebe ist grün
berlin   klust, piano   lp: dg LPEM 19 096
10-12
november
1956

o komme holde sommernacht
berlin   klust, piano   lp: dg LPEM 19 096
10-12
november
1956

o liebliche wangen
berlin   klust, piano   lp: dg LPEM 19 096
10-12
november
1956

ständchen (der mond steht über dem berge)
berlin   klust, piano   45: dg EPL 30 316
10-12   lp: dg LPEM 19 096
november
1956

tambourliebchen (den wirbel schlag' ich)
berlin   klust, piano   lp: dg LPEM 19 096
10-12
november
1956

unbewegte laue luft
berlin   klust, piano   lp: dg LPEM 19 096
10-12
november
1956

wenn du zuweilen lächelst
berlin   klust, piano   lp: dg LPEM 19 096
10-12
november
1956

wir wandelten wir zwei zusammen
berlin   klust, piano   lp: dg LPEM 19 096
10-12
november
1956
recordings for these brahms lieder were completed on 10 december 1956

BENJAMIN BRITTEN (1913-1976)
ernst haefliger took part in an unpublished wdr cologne recording of a spring symphony conducted by hans swarowsky

ANTON BRUCKNER (1824-1896)

mass no 3

munich	*tenor soloist*	lp: dg LPM 18 829/SLPM 138 829/
4-6	**jochum**	2720 054
july	bavarian radio	cd: dg 423 1272/447 4092
1962	orchestra	*excerpts*
	and chorus	lp: dg LPEM 19 491/SLPEM 136 491
	stader	
	hellmann	
	borg	

te deum

berlin	*tenor soloist*	lp: dg 139 117-139 118/136 552/139 999/
28 june-	**jochum**	2707 026/2720 054/2740 136
2 july	berlin	cd: dg 423 1272
1965	philharmonic	
	deutsche oper	
	chorus	
	stader	
	wagner	
	lagger	

ernst haefliger also took this part in an italian radio recording conducted by herbert von karajan and published by arkadia and urania

ALPHONS DIEPENBROCK (1862-1921)
ernst haefliger was the tenor soloist in a live performance of the te deum conducted by eduard van beinum and published by philips and donemus

ANTONIN DVORAK (1841-1904)

requiem
prague	*tenor soloist*	lp: dg LPM 18 547-18 548/
30 january-	**ancerl**	SLPM 138 026-138 027/2707 005
4 february	czech	cd: dg 437 3772
1959	philharmonic	*probably also published on the supraphon label*
	orchestra	
	and chorus	
	stader	
	wagner	
	borg	

CHRISTOPH WILLIBALD GLUCK (1714-1787)

iphigenie in aulis, excerpt (nur einen wunsch)
berlin	*role of pylades*	45: dg EPL 30 412
13 may	**könig**	
1957	rso berlin	

GEORGE FRIDERIC HANDEL (1685-1759)

brockes-passion
basel	*tenor soloist*	lp: dg archiv APM 14 418-14 420/
26 june-	**wenzinger**	SAPM 198 418-198 420/
9 july	schola cantorum	2710 006/413 9221
1961	basiliensis	cd: dg archiv 463 6442
	regensburg	*excerpts*
	cathedral choir	45: dg archiv EPA 37 223/SEPA 102 223
	stader	
	moser	
	esswood	
	jennings	
	adam	
	stämpfli	

giulio cesare, excerpt (svegliatevi nel core)
munich	*role of sesto*	lp: dg LPEM 19 268/SLPEM 136 268
5-6	**k.richter**	
august	munich bach	
1961	orchestra	

judas maccabaeus
berlin	*title role*	lp: dg LPEM 19 248-19 250/
november-	**koch**	139 248-139 250/2709 024
december	rundfunk-	lp: eterna
1966	orchester	cd: berlin classics BC 91122
	and chorus	*excerpts*
	janowitz	lp: dg 136 557
	töpper	
	schreier	
	adam	
	sung in german	

ernst haefliger also sang this work in a berlin radio performance conducted by ferenc fricsay and published by melodram

messiah
munich	*tenor soloist*	lp: dg LPM 18 051-18 953/
june	**k.richter**	SLPM 138 951-138 953/2709 015/
1964	munich bach	2721 076/413 9671
	orchestra	cd: dg 413 9672/439 7022
	and chorus	*excerpts*
	janowitz	lp: dg LPEM 19 476/SLPEM 136 476/
	höffgen	2535 745
	crass	
	sung in german	

samson, excerpt (total eclipse)
munich	*title role*	lp: dg LPEM 19 268/SLPEM 136 268
5-6	**k.richter**	
august	munich bach	
1961	orchestra	

serse, excerpts (se bramate d'amar; ombra mai fu)
munich	*title role*	lp: dg LPEM 19 268/SLPEM 136 268
5-6	**k.richter**	2535 745
august	munich bach	
1961	orchestra	

FRANZ JOSEF HAYDN (1732-1809)

die jahreszeiten
berlin   *tenor soloist*   lp: dg 2721 170
11 november   **fricsay**   *recorded at a public concert*
1961   rso berlin
    saint hedwig's
    choir
    stader
    greindl

nelson mass
budapest   *tenor soloist*   lp: dg LPEM 19 195/SLPEM 139 195
20-23   **ferencsik**   *probably also published on the hungaroton label*
june   hungarian
1966   state orchestra
    and chorus
    stader
    hellmann
    halem

ernst haefliger also took part in an unpublished swiss radio recording of die schöpfung conducted by karl richter

ARTHUR HONEGGER (1892-1955)
ernst haefliger takes part in an unpublished wdr cologne broadcast of le roi david conducted by hermann scherchen

LEOS JANACEK (1854-1928)

glagolithic mass
munich	*tenor soloist*	lp: dg LPM 18 954/SLPM 138 954/
november	**kubelik**	413 6521
1964	bavarian radio orchestra and chorus lear rössl-majdan crass	cd: dg 429 1822

the diary of one who disappeared
munich	kubelik, piano	lp: dg LPM 18 904/SLPM 138 904/
november	bavarian radio	2543 820
1963	chorus griffel	

ernst haefliger also recorded the work for philips accompanied by felix de nobel, and in an unpublished wdr cologne broadcast accompanied by gerhard puchelt

FERENC FRICSAY PORTRAIT

Zoltán Kodály

PSALMUS HUNGARICUS
SYMPHONIE
MAROSSZÉKER TÄNZE
Dances of Marosszék

Ernst Haefliger

RIAS-Symphonie-Orchester Berlin
Radio-Symphonie-Orchester Berlin

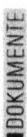
■ DOKUMENTE

ZOLTAN KODALY (1882-1967)

psalmus hungaricus
berlin	*tenor soloist*	lp: dg LPM 18 203-18 204/LPEM 19 073/
6-7	**fricsay**	2535 707
october	rso berlin	lp: decca (usa) DL 9773
1954	rias choir	

berlin	**fricsay**	cd: dg 445 4002/445 4102
29 september	rso berlin	*recorded at a public concert*
1959	saint hedwig's	
	choir	

ernst haefliger also recorded this part in an unpublished rai recording conducted by herbert von karajan, and in an unpublished wdr cologne recording conducted by ferdinand leitner

songs: gesang des verbannten; gleich dem feuer!; warte vöglein!
munich	klust, piano	lp: dg LPEM 19 171/SLPEM 136 017
22-26	*sung in german*	
august		
1958		

ALBERT LORTZING (1801-1851)

der wildschütz, excerpt (ihr weib? mein teures weib!)
bamberg	*role of baron*	lp: dg LPEM 19 428/SLPEM 136 428/
19-22	**stepp**	2535 429/410 8741
september	bamberg so	lp: dg heliodor 2548 120
1965	seefried	cd: dg 437 6772

der wildchütz, excerpts (ich habe numero eins; was seh' ich?)
bamberg	*role of baron*	lp: dg LPEM 19 428/SLPEM 136 428/
19-22	**stepp**	2535 429
september	bamberg so	lp: dg heliodor 2548 120
1965	prague	
	philharmonic	
	choir	
	seefried	
	streich	
	hellmann	
	günter	
	böhme	

Deutsche Grammophon Gesellschaft

GUSTAV MAHLER
(1860—1911)

Das Lied von der Erde
(The Song of the Earth)

Text by Hans Bethge from "The Chinese Flute"

SIDE 1

Das Trinklied vom Jammer der Erde (Tenor)
(Drinking Song of the Misery of the World)

Der Einsame im Herbst (Alt)
(Loneliness in Autumn)

Von der Jugend (Tenor)
(Song of Youth)

Von der Schönheit (Alt)
(Song of Beauty)

Der Trunkene im Frühling (Tenor)
(The Drunkard in Spring)

SIDE 2

Der Abschied (Alt)
(The Parting)

Nan Merriman, Mezzo-Soprano · Ernst Haefliger, Tenor
Concertgebouworkest Amsterdam
Conductor: Eugen Jochum

Artistic Supervision: Wolfgang Lohse · Recording Engineer: Heinz Waldhagen

18 865 HI-FI · 138 865 STEREO

GUILLAUME DE MACHAUT (1300-1377)

messe nostre dame
wettingen 17-20 october 1969	*tenor soloist* **wenzinger** schola cantorum basiliensis melzer stämpfli widmer	lp: dg archiv 2533 054

virelai no 17
wettingen 17-20 october 1969	**wenzinger** schola cantorum basiliensis	lp: dg archiv 2533 054

ballades nos 16, 18, 26 and 39
wettingen 17-20 october 1969	**wenzinger** schola cantorum basiliensis	lp: dg archiv 2533 054

rondeaux nos 1, 10 and 21
wettingen 17-20 october 1969	**wenzinger** schola cantorum basiliensis	lp: dg archiv 2533 054

GUSTAV MAHLER (1869-1911)

das lied von der erde
amsterdam 26 march- 2 april 1963	*tenor soloist* **jochum** concertgebouw orchestra merriman	lp: dg LPM 18 865/SLPM 138 865/ 2535 184 cd: dg 439 4712

ernst haefliger also recorded this part for american columbia conducted by bruno walter and for philips conducted by eduard van beinum, and in an unpublished wdr cologne broadcast conducted by hans rosbaud

FRANK MARTIN (1890-1974)
ernst haefliger was the tenor soloist in a decca recording of the oratorio in terra pax, conducted by ernest ansermet

JULES MASSENET (1842-1912)

manon, excerpts (en fermant les yeux; ah fuyez douce image!)
berlin   *role of des grieux*   45: dg EPL 30 591
29-30   **märzendorfer**
may   rso berlin
1961   *sung in german*

WOLFGANG AMADEUS MOZART (1756-1791)

cosi fan tutte
berlin	*role of ferrando*	lp: dg LPM 18 861-18 863/
8-17	**jochum**	SLPM 138 861-138 863/2709 012/
december	berlin	2728 010
1962	philharmonic	cd: dg 449 5802
	rias choir	*excerpts*
	seefried	lp: dg LPM 18 792/SLPM 138 792/
	merriman	136 278/135 004/2537 019
	köth	
	prey	
	fischer-dieskau	

don giovanni
berlin	*role of ottavio*	lp: dg LPM 18 850-18 852/
september-	**fricsay**	SLPM 138 050-138 052/2728 003/
october	rso berlin	lp: dg heliodor 2730 014
1958	rias choir	cd: dg 437 3412/463 6292
	stader	*excerpts*
	jurinac	lp: dg LPEM 19 224/SLPEM 136 224
	seefried	
	fischer-dieskau	
	kohn	
	kreppel	

don giovanni, excerpts (dalla sua pace; il mio tesoro)
berlin	*role of ottavio*	lp: dg LPEM 19 415/SLPEM 136 415/
february	**löwlein**	2535 745
1963	rso berlin	cd: dg 447 8122
	sung in german	

don giovanni, excerpt (non ti fidar o misera)
berlin	*role of ottavio*	lp: dg LPEM 19 415/SLPEM 136 415
february	**löwlein**	cd: dg 447 8122
1963	rso berlin	
	watson	
	salemka	
	fischer-dieskau	
	sung in german	

don giovanni, excerpt (don ottavio son morta!)
berlin	*role of ottavio*	lp: dg LPEM 19 415/SLPEM 136 415
february	**löwlein**	
1963	rso berlin	
	watson	
	sung in german	

die entführung aus dem serail
berlin	*role of belmonte*	lp: dg LPM 18 184-18 185/
16-24	**fricsay**	LPM 18 197-18 198
may	rso berlin	lp: dg heliodor 89 756-89 757/2700 010/
1954	rias choir	2730 014
	stader	lp: decca (usa) DX 133
	streich	cd: dg 437 7302/445 4122
	vantin	*excerpts*
	greindl	45: dg EPL 30 139/EPL 30 140/
		NL 32 093/NL 32 095
		lp: dg LPE 17 113/LPM 18 558-18 559

die zauberflöte

berlin	*role of tamino*	lp: dg LPM 18 264-18 266/
june	**fricsay**	LPM 18 267-18 269/2728 009
1955	rso berlin	lp: dg heliodor 89 662-89 664/2701 003/
	rias choir	2730 014
	stader	lp: decca (usa) DX 134
	streich	lp: philips 6747 387
	otto	lp: eterna 820 226-820 228
	schech	cd: dg 437 7412/459 4972
	klose	*excerpts*
	vantin	45: dg EPL 30 237/NL 32 143
	fischer-dieskau	lp: dg LPM 18 558-18 559
	greindl	lp: dg heliodor 89 653
	borg	

coronation mass

paris	*tenor soloist*	lp: dg LPE 17 222/LPM 18 631/
7-8	**markevitch**	SLPE 133 222/SLPM 138 131/
december	lamoureux	136 511/2535 148
1959	orchestra	cd: dg 429 5102/457 7442
	brasseur choir	*excerpts*
	stader	lp: dg LPEM 19 491/SLPEM 136 491
	dominguez	
	roux	

OTTO NICOLAI (1810-1849)

die lustigen weiber von windsor, excerpt (horch die lerche singt im hain)

bamberg	*role of fenton*	45: dg EPL 30 591
3-8	**löwlein**	lp: dg LPEM 19 421/SLPEM 136 421
march	bamberg	
1964	symphony	

LUIGI NONO (1924-1990)

ernst haefliger takes part in an unpublished wdr cologne recording of sul ponte di hiroshima conducted by bruno maderna

CARL ORFF (1895-1982)

antigonae
munich
25 march-
16 april
1961

role of tiresias
leitner
bavarian radio
orchestra
and chorus
borkh
hellmann
plümacher
stolze
uhl
borg
alexander

lp: dg LPM 18 717-18 719/
SLPM 138 717-138 719/2709 009/
2740 226
cd: dg 437 7212

GIAOCCHINO ROSSINI (1792-1868)

stabat mater
berlin
16-19
september
1954

tenor soloist
fricsay
rso berlin
rias and saint
hedwig's choirs
stader
radev
borg

lp: dg LPM 18 203-18 204/LPM 18340/
2535 718
lp: dg heliodor 89 610/2548 126
lp: decca (usa) DX 132
cd: dg 439 6842
excerpts
45: dg EPL 30 139

il barbiere di siviglia, excerpt (ecco ridente in cielo)
berlin
20-24
april
1964

role of almaviva
peters
deutsche oper
orchestra
sung in german

lp: dg LPEM 19 423/SLPEM 136 423/
2535 374/2535 745

il barbiere di siviglia, excerpt (all' idea di quel metallo)

berlin	*role of almaviva*	lp: dg LPEM 19 423/SLPEM 136 423/
20-24	**peters**	2535 374/2535 745
april	deutsche oper	
1964	orchestra	
	grumbach	
	sung in german	

il barbiere di siviglia, excerpt (ah quel colpo inaspettato!)

berlin	*role of almaviva*	lp: dg LPEM 19 423/SLPEM 136 423/
20-24	**peters**	2535 374
april	deutsche oper	
1964	orchestra	
	streich	
	grumbach	
	sung in german	

il barbiere di siviglia, excerpt (amor e fede eterna!)

berlin	*role of almaviva*	lp: dg LPEM 19 423/SLPEM 136 423/
20-24	**peters**	2535 374
april	deutsche oper	
1964	orchestra	
	rias choir	
	streich	
	grumbach	
	sardi	
	borg	
	sung in german	

OTHMAR SCHOECK (1886-1957)

lieder: wanderlied der prager studenten; an meine mutter; nachruf; das bescheidene wünschlein

munich	klust, piano	lp: dg LPEM 19 171/SLPEM 136 017
20-22		
august		
1958		

ernst haefliger also recorded lieder by schoeck for the swiss label claves

FRANZ SCHUBERT (11797-1828)

mass in a flat
regensburg   *tenor soloist*   lp: dg 139 108
11-14   **ratzinger**
july   bavarian radio
1965   orchestra
     regensburg
     cathedral choir
     stader
     höffgen
     uhde

die schöne müllerin, song cycle
munich   bonneau, piano   lp: dg LPEM 19 207-19 208/
16-29   SLPEM 136 039-136 040/2538 001
august   *excerpts*
1959   lp: dg 135 005

schwanengesang, song cycle
vienna   werba, piano   lp: dg LPM 18 905/SLPM 138 905/
1965   410 5441

abschied *see schwanengesang*

am feierabend *see die schöne müllerin*

am meer *see schwanengesang*

an den mond (geuss lieber mond)
berlin   klust, piano   lp: dg LPEM 19 096
10-12
november
1956

an die laute (leiser leiser kleine laute)
berlin   klust, piano   45: dg EPL 30 316
10-12   lp: dg LPEM 19 096
november
1956

an silvia (was ist silvia?)
berlin   klust, piano   lp: dg LPEM 19 096
10-12
november
1956

der atlas *see schwanengesang*

aufenthalt *see schwanengesang*

des baches wiegenlied *see die schöne müllerin*

die böse farbe *see die schöne müllerin*

danksagung an den bach *see die schöne müllerin*

der doppelgänger *see schwanengesang*

eifersucht und stolz *see die schöne müllerin*

das fischermädchen *see schwanengesang*

frühlingssehnsucht *see schwanengesang*

halt! *see die schöne müllerin*

ihr bild *see schwanengesang*

in der ferne *see schwanengesang*

der jäger *see die schöne müllerin*

der jüngling an der quelle (leise rieselnder quell)
berlin   klust, piano   45: dg EPL 30 316
10-12   lp: dg LPEM 19 096
november
1956

kriegers ahnung *see schwanengesang*

Die Entführung aus dem Serail

Wolfgang Amadè Mozart

Deutsche Grammophon Gesellschaft

die liebe farbe *see die schöne müllerin*

liebesbotschaft *see schwanengesang*

mein! *see die schöne müllerin*

mit dem grünen lautenbande *see die schöne müllerin*

morgengruss *see die schöne müllerin*

der müller und das bach *see die schöne müllerin*

des müllers blumen *see die schöne müllerin*

der musensohn (durch feld und wald zu schweifen)
berlin   klust, piano   45: dg EPL 30 316
10-12   lp: dg LPEM 19 096
november
1956

der neugierige *see die schöne müllerin*

pause *see die schöne müllerin*

rastlose liebe (dem schnee dem regen)
berlin   klust, piano   lp: dg LPEM 19 096
10-12
november
1956

sei mir gegrüsst (o du entriss'ne mir)
berlin   klust, piano   lp: dg LPEM 19 096
10-12
november
1956

sprache der liebe (lass dich mit gelinden schlägen rühren)
berlin klust, piano lp: dg LPEM 19 096
10-12
november
1956

die stadt *see schwanengesang*

ständchen *see schwanengesang*

stimme der liebe (meine selinde!)
berlin klust, piano lp: dg LPEM 19 096
10-12
november
1956

die taubenpost *see schwanengesang*

tränenregen *see die schöne müllerin*

trockne blumen *see die schöne müllerin*

ungeduld *see die schöne müllerin*

das wandern *see die schöne müllerin*

wohin? *see die schöne müllerin*

wonne der wehmut (trocknet nicht tränen der ewigen liebe)
berlin klust, piano lp: dg LPEM 19 096
10-12
november
1956

ernst haefliger also recorded schubert lieder for the swiss label claves

ROBERT SCHUMANN (1810-1856)

dichterliebe, song cycle
berlin   werba, piano   lp: dg LPM 18 843/SLPM 138 843
5-12
october
1962

an den mond (schlafloser sonne melancholischer stern)
munich   bonneau, piano   lp: dg LPEM 19 207-19 208/
august   SLPEM 136 039-136 040
1959

an den sonnenschein (o sonnenschein wie scheinst du)
munich   bonneau, piano   lp: dg LPEM 19 207-19 208/
august   SLPEM 136 039-136 040/135 007
1959

aus alten märchen winkt es *see dichterliebe*

das ist ein flöten und geigen *see dichterliebe*

geisternähe (was weht um meine schläfe?)
munich   bonneau, piano   lp: dg LPEM 19 207-19 208/
august   SLPEM 136 039-136 040
1959

der himmel hat eine träne geweinet
munich   bonneau, piano   lp: dg LPEM 19 207-19 208/
august   SLPEM 136 039-136 040
1959

hör' ich das liedchen klingen *see dichterliebe*

ich grolle nicht *see dichterliebe*

ich hab' im traum geweinet *see dichterliebe*

ich wandelte unter den bäumen/liederkreis op 24
munich   bonneau, piano   lp: dg LPEM 19 207-19 208/
august   SLPEM 136 039-136 040
1959

ich will meine seele tauchen *see dichterliebe*

im rhein im heiligen strome *see dichterliebe*

im wunderschönen monat mai *see dichterliebe*

ins freie (mir ist's so eng allüberall)
munich   bonneau, piano   lp: dg LPEM 19 207-19 208/
august   SLPEM 136 039-136 040
1959

ein jüngling liebt ein mädchen *see dichterliebe*

der knabe mit dem wunderhorn (ich bin ein lust'ger geselle)
munich   klust, piano   lp: dg LPEM 19 171/SLPEM 136 017
20-22
august
1958

lieb liebchen leg's händchen aufs herze mein/liederkreis op 24
munich   bonneau, piano   lp: dg LPEM 19 207-19 208/
august   SLPEM 136 039-136 040
1959

märzveilchen (der himmel wölbt sich rein und blau)
munich   bonneau, piano   lp: dg LPEM 19 207-19 208/
august   SLPEM 136 039-136 040
1959

meine rose (dem holden lenzgeschmeide)
munich   klust, piano   lp: dg LPEM 19 171/SLPEM 136 017
20-22
august
1958

mondnacht/liederkreis op 39
munich   klust, piano   lp: dg LPEM 19 171/SLPEM 136 017
20-22
august
1958

der nussbaum (es grünet ein nussbaum vor dem haus)
munich   klust, piano   lp: dg LPEM 19 171/SLPEM 136 017
20-22
august
1958

die rose die lilie *see dichterliebe*

sängers trost
munich   bonneau, piano   lp: dg LPEM 19 207-19 208/
august   SLPEM 136 039-136 040
1959

schöne fremde/liederkreis op 39
munich   klust, piano   lp: dg LPEM 19 171/SLPEM 136 017
20-22
august
1958

schöne wiege meiner leiden/liederkreis op 24
munich   bonneau, piano   lp: dg LPEM 19 207-19 208/
august   SLPEM 136 039-136 040
1959

und wüssten's die blumen *see dichterliebe*

wenn ich in deine augen seh' *see dichterliebe*

ernst haefliger also recorded schumann lieder for the swiss label claves

IGOR STRAVINSKY (1882-1971)
ernst haefliger took part in a recording of les noces for philips, accompanied by felix de nobel

GEORG PHILIPP TELEMANN (1681-1767)

der getreue musikmeister
nürnberg   *tenor soloist*   lp: dg archiv 198 425-198 429/2714 002/
16-30   **ulsamer**   2723 053
august   ulsamer   *excerpts*
1966   collegium   lp: dg archiv 199 019
                mathis   *recordings completed in april 1967*
                töpper
                sommer
                unger
                mcdaniel

AMBROISE THOMAS (1811-1896)

mignon, excerpts (adieu mignon couage!; elle est la! elle est aimée; elle ne croyait pas)

paris 15-19 november 1963	*role of wilhelm* **fournet** lamoureux orchestra *sung in german*	lp: dg LPEM 19 418/SLPEM 136 418

GIUSEPPE VERDI (1813-1901)

la traviata, excerpt (libiamo ne lieti calici)

harburg 15-17 february 1958	*role of alfredo* **schmidt- isserstedt** ndr orchestra and chorus *sung in german*	45: dg EPL 30 606/SEPL 121 606 lp: dg LPEM 19 139/SLPEM 136 005/ 2535 745 lp: dg heliodor 2548 117

la traviata, excerpt (un di felice)

harburg 15-17 february 1958	*role of alfredo* **schmidt- isserstedt** ndr orchestra stader *sung in german*	lp: dg LPEM 19 139/SLPEM 136 005 lp: dg heliodor 2548 117

la traviata, excerpt (parigi o cara)

harburg 15-17 february 1958	*role of alfredo* **schmidt- isserstedt** ndr orchestra stader *sung in german*	45: dg EPL 30 606/SEPL 121 606 lp: dg LPEM 19 139/SLPEM 136 005 lp: dg heliodor 2548 117

la traviata, excerpt (prendi quest' e l'immagine)

harburg	*role of alfredo*	lp: dg LPEM 19 139/SLPEM 136 005
15-17	**schmidt-**	lp: dg heliodor 2548 117
february	**isserstedt**	
1958	ndr orchestra	
	stader	
	winters	
	sung in german	

la traviata, excerpt (act 2 finale)

harburg	*role of alfredo*	lp: dg LPEM 19 139/SLPEM 136 005
15-17	**schmidt-**	lp: dg heliodor 2548 117
february	**isserstedt**	
1958	ndr orchestra	
	and chorus	
	stader	
	zollenkopf	
	winters	
	sellentin	
	stuckmann	
	sung in german	

the excerpts from la traviata were recorded as part of a continuous querschnitt

RICHARD WAGNER (1813-1883)

der fliegende holländer

berlin	*role of steuermann*	lp: dg LPM 18 063-18 065/
october	**fricsay**	LPM 18 116-18 118
1952	rso berlin	lp: dg heliodor 2701 009
	rias choir	lp: decca (usa) DX 124
	kupper	cd: dg 439 7142
	wagner	*excerpts*
	windgassen	lp: dg LPEM 19 015/LPEM 19 122
	metternich	
	greindl	

HUGO WOLF (1860-1903)

auf einer wanderung/mörike-lieder
munich   klust, piano   lp: dg LPEM 19 171/SLPEM 136 017
20-22
august
1958

er ist's/mörike-lieder
munich   klust, piano   lp: dg LPEM 19 171/SLPEM 136 017/
20-22   135 007
august
1958

der gärtner/mörike-lieder
munich   klust, piano   lp: dg LPEM 19 171/SLPEM 136 017
20-22
august
1958

heimweh/mörike-lieder
munich   klust, piano   lp: dg LPEM 19 171/SLPEM 136 017
20-22
august
1958

in der frühe/mörike-lieder
munich   klust, piano   lp: dg LPEM 19 171/SLPEM 136 017
20-22
august
1958

MISCELLANEOUS
ernst haefliger recorded an lp of old german christmas carols conducted by paul angerer and published by claves

josef greindl
1912-1993

LUDWIG VAN BEETHOVEN (1770-1827)

missa solemnis

berlin	*bass soloist*	lp: dg LPM 18 224-18 225/
3-12	**böhm**	LPM 18 232-18 233
january	berlin	lp: dg heliodor 89 679-89 680
1955	philharmonic	lp: decca (usa) DX 135
	saint hedwig's	cd: dg 449 7372
	choir	*also unofficially issued in an incorrectly dated lp*
	stader	*edition by discocorp*
	radev	
	dermota	

josef greindl is also bass soloist in a wdr cologne performance of missa solemnis conducted by ptto klemperer and published by movimento musica/frequenz

josef greindl also sings the role of rocco in live performances of fidelio conducted by wilhelm furtwängler published by emi and other labels, conducted by ernest ansermet published by melodram, and in an unpublished hamburg staatsoper film of the opera conducted by karl böhm

ALBAN BERG (1885-1935)

lulu

berlin	*role of schigolch*	lp: dg 139 273-139 275/2709 029/
february	**böhm**	413 7971/413 8071
1968	deutsche oper	cd: dg 435 7052
	orchestra	
	lear	
	johnson	
	driscoll	
	feldhoff	
	fischer-dieskau	

PETER CORNELIUS (1824-1874)

josef greindl recorded several songs by this composer in 1943 and 1944 for reichsrundfunk accompanied by michael raucheisen and subsequently published by basf/acanta

GAETONO DONIZETTI (1797-1848)

don pasquale, excerpt (ah un foco insolito)
munich *title role* lp: dg LPE 17 053
1-6 **lehmann**
february bavarian radio
1954 orchestra
sung in german

FRIEDRICH VON FLOTOW (1812-1883)

martha
berlin *role of plumkett* lp: dg LPEM 19 253-19 254
october **schüler** lp: dg heliodor 2700 110
1944 staatskapelle *originally a reichsrundfunk recording published by*
 and chorus *urania and subsequently also issued by eterna,*
 berger *basf/acanta, fonoteam, berlin classics and*
 tegethoff *phonographe*
 anders
 fuchs

CHRISTOPH WILLIBALD GLUCK (1714-1787)
josef greindl sings the role of kalchas in a berlin radio performance of iphigenie in aulis conducted by artur rother and published by melodram and gala

CHARLES GOUNOD (1818-1893)

faust, excerpt (le veau d'or)
munich *role of mephisto* 78: dg L 62 887
3 february **rieger** 45: dg EPL 30 007
1952 munich lp: preiser 135021
 philharmonic cd: preiser 90124
 sung in german

faust, excerpt (vous qui faites l'emdormie)
munich *role of mephisto* 78: dg L 62 887
3 february **rieger** 45: dg EPL 30 007
1952 munich lp: dg LPEM 19 043
 philharmonic
 sung in german

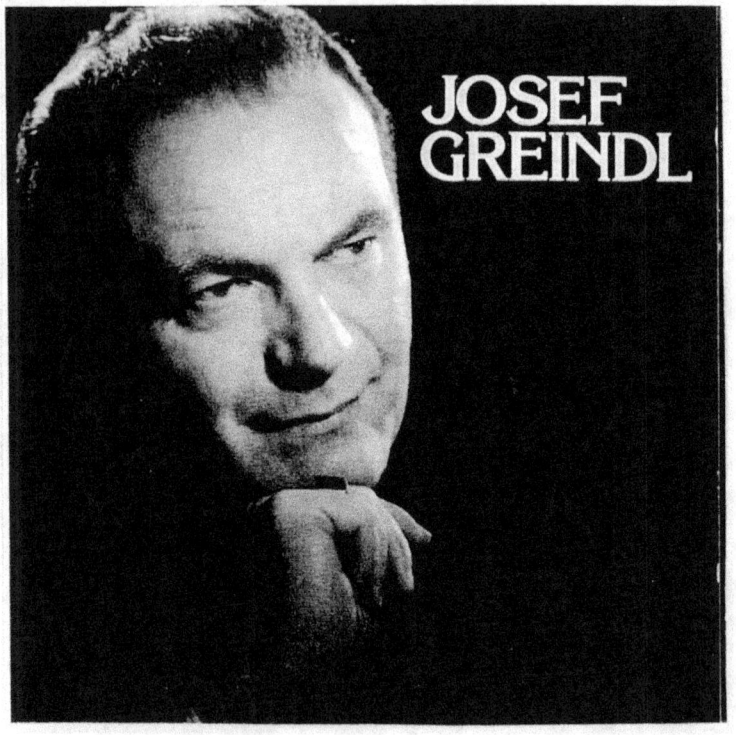

JACQUES HALEVY (1799-1862)

la juive, excerpt (si la rigueur)
berlin	*role of brogny*	45: dg NL 32 116
18 november	**ludwig**	lp: dg LPE 17 081
1955	rso berlin	cd: preiser 90124
	sung in german	

FRANZ JOSEF HAYDN (1732-1809)

saint cecilia mass
munich	*bass soloist*	lp: dg LPM 18 545-18 546/
10-12	**jochum**	SLPM 138 028-138 029
october	bavarian radio	cd: dg 437 3832/445 0522
1958	orchestra	
	and chorus	
	stader	
	höffgen	
	holm	

die jahreszeiten
berlin	*bass soloist*	lp: dg LPM 18 025-18028/
21-28	**fricsay**	LPM 18 486-18 488
january	rso berlin	lp: dg heliodor 2701 010
1952	saint hedwig's	lp: decca (usa) DX 123
	and rias choirs	cd: dg 474 3832
	trötschel	*excerpts*
	w.ludwig	78: dg L 62 895
		45: dg NL 32 217

berlin	**fricsay**	lp: dg 2721 170
11 november	rso berlin	*recorded at a public concert*
1961	saint hedwig's	
	choir	
	stader	
	haefliger	

josef greindl also took part in an unpublished wdr cologne broadcast of die schöpfung conducted by joseph keilberth

CARL LOEWE (1796-1869)

archibald douglas (ich hab' es getragen sieben jahr)
berlin klust, piano 78: dg LVM 72 102
11 january lp: dg LP 16 010/LPE 17 138/29 258
1951 cd: dg 457 0182

edward (dein schwert wie ist's vom blut so rot?)
berlin klust, piano 78: dg LVM 72 063
11 january lp: dg LP 16 010/LPE 17 138/29 258
1951 lp: decca (usa) DL 9610
cd: dg 457 0182

erlkönig (wer reitet so spät durch nacht und wind?)
berlin klust, piano 45: dg EPL 30 676/SEPL 121 676
6-10 lp: dg LPEM 19 239/SLPEM 136 239
march cd: dg 449 3522
1961 cd: preiser 90295

der heilige franziskus (franziskus einst der heil'ge sass)
berlin klust, piano lp: dg LP 16 100/LPE 17 041/29 258
28-30 cd: dg 457 0182
may cd: preiser 90295
1954

heinrich der vogler (herr heinrich sitzt am vogelherd)
berlin klust, piano 45: dg EPL 30 207
28-30 lp: dg LP 16 100/LPE 17 041/29 258
may cd: dg 457 0182
1954 cd: preiser 90295

die heinzelmännchen (wie war zu köln es doch vordem)
berlin klust, piano lp: dg LPEM 19 239/SLPEM 136 239
6-10 cd: dg 449 3522
march cd: preiser 90295
1961

herr oluf reitet spät und weit
berlin   klust, piano   lp: dg LPEM 19 239/SLPEM 136 239
6-10   cd: dg 449 3522
march   cd: preiser 90295
1961

hinkende jamben (ein liebchen hatt' ich)
berlin   klust, piano   lp: dg LPEM 19 239/SLPEM 136 239
6-10   cd: dg 449 3522
march   cd: preiser 90295
1961

hochzeitlied (wir singen und sagen vom grafen)
berlin   klust, piano   45: dg EPL 30 676/SEPL 121 676
6-10   lp: dg LPEM 19 239/SLPEM 136 239
march   cd: dg 449 3522
1961   cd: preiser 90295

kleiner haushalt (einen haushalt klein und fein)
berlin   klust, piano   lp: dg LPEM 19 239/SLPEM 136 239
6-10   cd: dg 449 3522
march   cd: preiser 90295
1961

mädchen sind wie der wind
berlin   klust, piano   lp: dg LPEM 19 239/SLPEM 136 239
6-10   cd: dg 449 3522
march   cd: preiser 90295
1961

meeresleuchten (wieviel sonnenstrahlen fielen goldenschwer)
berlin   klust, piano   lp: dg LPEM 19 239/SLPEM 136 239
6-10   cd: dg 449 3522
march   cd: preiser 90295
1961

der mohrenfürst (sein heer durchwogte das palmental)
berlin	klust, piano	lp: dg LPEM 19 239/SLPEM 136 239
6-10		cd: dg 449 3522
march		cd: preiser 90295
1961		

der nöck (es tönt des nöcken harfenschall)
berlin	klust, piano	78: dg LVM 72 063
11 january		lp: dg LP 16 010/LPE 17 138/29 258
1951		lp: decca (usa) DL 9610
		cd: dg 457 0182

ödins meeresritt (meister oluf der schmied von helgoland)
berlin	klust, piano	45: dg EPL 30 676/SEPL 121 676
6-10		lp: dg LPEM 19 239/SLPEM 136 239
march		cd: dg 449 3522
1961		cd: preiser 90295

prinz eugen der edle ritter
berlin	klust, piano	45: dg EPL 30 207
28-30		lp: dg LP 16 100/LPE 17 041/29 258
may		cd: dg 457 0182
1954		cd: preiser 90295

schwalbenmärchen (auf dem stillen schwülen pfuhle)
berlin	klust, piano	lp: dg LPEM 19 239/SLPEM 136 239
6-10		cd: dg 449 3522
march		cd: preiser 90295
1961		

spirito santo (in des südens heissen zonen)
berlin	klust, piano	lp: dg LP 16 100/LPE 17 041/29 258
28-30		cd: dg 449 3522
may		cd: preiser 90295
1954		

süsses begräbnis (schäferin ach wir haben sie dich so süss begraben)
berlin	klust, piano	lp: dg LPEM 19 239/SLPEM 136 239
6-10		cd: dg 449 3522
march		cd: preiser 90295
1961		

tom der reimer (der reimer thomas lag am bach)
berlin	klust, piano	45: dg EPL 30 208/LPHM 46 894
28-30		lp: dg LP 16 100/LPE 17 041/29 258
may		cd: dg 457 0182
1954		cd: preiser 90295

die uhr (ich trage wo ich gehe stets eine uhr bei mir)
berlin	klust, piano	78: dg AVM 9100
28-30		45: dg EPL 30 208/LPHM 46 895
may		lp: dg LP 16 100/LPE 17 041/29 258
1954		cd: dg 457 0182
		cd: preiser 90295

die verfallene mühle (es reitet schweigend und allein)
berlin	klust, piano	lp: dg LPEM 19 239/SLPEM 136 239
6-10		cd: dg 449 3522
march		cd: preiser 90295
1961		

josef greindl also recorded a group of loewe ballads for the reichsrundfunk in 1943 and 1944, accompanied by michael raucheisen and subsequently published by basf/acanta

ALBERT LORTZING

Der Waffenschmied

Gundula Janowitz
Sieglinde Wagner
Josef Greindl
Thomas Stewart
Martin Vantin

Dirigent:
Christoph Stepp

ALBERT LORTZING (1801-1851)

der waffenschmied, excerpt (auch ich war ein jüngling mit lockigem haar)
berlin	*role of stadinger*	lp: dg LPEM 19 417/SLPEM 136 417/
3-5	**stepp**	2535 299
december	rso berlin	cd: dg 447 8142
1963		

der waffenschmied, excerpts (bei nächt'gem dunkel; gern gäb' ich glanz und reichtum hin)
berlin	*role of stadinger*	lp: dg LPEM 19 417/SLPEM 136 417/
3-5	**stepp**	2535 299
december	rso berlin	cd: dg 447 8142
1963	rias choir	
	janowitz	
	wagner	
	vantin	
	stewart	

WOLFGANG AMADEUS MOZART (1756-1791)

don giovanni, excerpt (madamina!)
berlin	*role of leporello*	78: dg LVM 72 482
5 february	**lehmann**	45: dg EPL 30 078
1954	rso berlin	lp: dg LPM 18 558-18 559

berlin	**lehmann**	45: dg EPL 30 077
5 february	rso berlin	lp: dg LPE 17 014
1954	*sung in german*	

josef greindl sings the role of the commendatore in a salzburg festival performance of don giovanni conducted by wilhelm furtwängler and published by emi and other labels

die entführung aus dem serail

berlin	*role of osmin*	lp: dg LPM 18 184-18 185/
16-24	**fricsay**	LPM 18 197-18 198
may	rso berlin	lp: dg heliodor 89 756-89 757/
1954	rias choir	2700 010/2730 014
	stader	lp: decca (usa) DX 133
	streich	cd: dg 437 7302/445 4122
	haefliger	*excerpts*
	vantin	45: dg EPL 30 274/NL 32 096
		lp: dg LPE 17 113/LPEM 19321/ LPEM 19 409
		lp: dg heliodor 89 653

josef greindl also sings the role of osmin in a berlin radio performance also conducted by ferenc fricsay and published by movimento musica and myto

le nozze di figaro, excerpt (non piu andrai)

munich	*role of figaro*	45: dg NL 32 070
1 february	**lehmann**	lp: decca (usa) DL 4065
1952	munich philharmonic	

munich	**lehmann**	78: dg LV 36 025
1 february	munich	45: dg NL 32 069
1952	philharmonic	lp: dg LPM 18 147/LPEM 19 043/ LPEM 19 066
	sung in german	lp: dg heliodor 89 539
		cd: preiser 90124

le nozze di figaro, excerpt (aprite un po quegli' occhi!)

munich	*role of figaro*	45: dg NL 32 070
1 february	**lehmann**	lp: dg LPM 18 558-18 559
1952	munich philharmonic	lp: decca (usa) DL 4065

munich	**lehmann**	78: dg LV 36 025
1 february	munich	45: dg NL 32 069
1952	philharmonic	lp: dg LPEM 19 066
	sung in german	lp: dg heliodor 89 539

die zauberflöte
berlin	*role of sarastro*	lp: dg LPM 18 264-18 266/
june	**fricsay**	LPM 18 267-18 269/2728 009
1955	rso berlin	lp: dg heliodor 89 662-89 664/
	rias choir	2701 003/2730 014
	stader	lp: decca (usa) DX 134
	streich	lp: philips 6747 387
	otto	lp: eterna 820 226-820 228
	schech	cd: dg 437 7412/459 4972
	klose	*excerpts*
	haefliger	lp: dg LPEM 19 015/LPEM 19 194
	vantin	
	fischer-dieskau	
	borg	

josef greindl also sings the role of sarastro in salzburg festival performances conducted by wilhelm furtwängler and published by emi and other labels

die zauberflöte, excerpt (in diesen heil'gen hallen)
berlin	*role of sarastro*	45: dg NL 32 071
14 february	**lehmann**	lp: dg LPE 17 081/LPEM 19 015
1954	rso berlin	

die zauberflöte, excerpt (o isis und osiris)
berlin	*role of sarastro*	45: dg NL 32 071
14 february	**lehmann**	cd: preiser 90124
1954	rso berlin	
	rias choir	

coronation mass
berlin	*bass soloist*	lp: dg LP 16 096/LPE 17 141/29 330
18-21	**markevitch**	lp: decca (usa) DL 9805
february	berlin	cd: dg 437 3832
1954	philharmonic	
	saint hedwig's	
	choir	
	stader	
	wagner	
	krebs	

MODEST MUSSORGSKY (1839-1881)

boris godunov, excerpt (i have attained the highest power)
munich
2 february
1952
title role
lehmann
munich
philharmonic
sung in german
45: dg EPL 30 007/EPL 30 102
lp: dg LPE 17 081
cd: preiser 90124

boris godunov, excerpt (death of boris)
munich
2 february
1952
title role
lehmann
munich
philharmonic
sung in german
78: dg LV 36 039
45: dg EPL 30 414
lp: preiser 135021
cd: preiser 90124

OTTO NICOLAI (1810-1849)

josef greindl recorded several songs by this composer for the reichsrundfunk accompanied by michael raucheisen and subsequently published by basf/acanta

CARL ORFF (1895-1982)

de temporum fine comoedia
leverkusen
16-21
july
1973
bass soloist
karajan
wdr orchestra
and chorus
rias choir
ludwig
schreier
lp: dg 2530 432
cd: dg 429 8592

josef greindl sings the same part in an unpublished salzburg festival radio broadcast also conducted by herbert von karajan; he also sings the role of kratos in a cologne radio broadcast of orff's prometheus conducted by ferdinand leitner and published by rca and basf/acanta, and the role of messenger in a salzburg festival performance of antigonae conducted by ferenc fricsay and published by stradivarius

FRANZ SCHUBERT (1797-1828)

winterreise, song cycle
hannover klust, piano lp: dg LPEM 19 093-19 094
16-19 cd: dg 457 0182
january cd: preiser 90128
1957 *excerpts*
 lp: dg LPEM 19 155

an die leier (ich will von atreus söhnen)
berlin klust, piano lp: dg LPEM 19 093-19 094
3-9 cd: dg 457 0182
march
1957

an die musik (du holde kunst in wieviel grauen stunden)
berlin klust, piano lp: dg LPEM 19 093-19 094
3-9 cd: dg 457 0182
march
1957

auf dem flusse *see winterreise*

aufenthalt/schwanengesang
berlin klust, piano lp: dg LPEM 19 093-19 094
3-9 cd: dg 457 0182
march
1957

einsamkeit *see winterreise*

erstarrung *see winterreise*

frühlingstraum *see winterreise*

gefror'ne tränen *see winterreise*

der greise kopf *see winterreise*

gute nacht *see winterreise*

im dorfe *see winterreise*

irrlicht *see winterreise*

die krähe *see winterreise*

der leiermann *see winterreise*

letzte hoffnung *see winterreise*

der lindenbaum *see winterreise*

mut *see winterreise*

die nebensonnen *see winterreise*

die post *see winterreise*

rast *see winterreise*

rückblick *see winterreise*

sehnsucht (ach aus dieses tales gründen)
berlin	klust, piano	lp: dg LPEM 19 093-19 094
3-9		cd: dg 457 0182
march		
1957		

EXTENDED PLAY 45

ARCHIV
PRODUKTION
DES MUSIKHISTORISCHEN STUDIOS DER DEUTSCHEN GRAMMOPHON GESELLSCHAFT

VI. FORSCHUNGSBEREICH
Deutsche Barockmusik
SERIE A: HEINRICH SCHÜTZ

2 Symphoniae sacrae
Fili mi, Absalon
Attendite

Josef Greindl, Baß
Willy Wobbe, Posaune / Johann Klaus, Posaune / Bruno Jaenen, Tenor-Posaune
Franz Herbert, Posaune / Klaus Juncker/Bottrop, Orgelpositiv

37012 EPA

täuschung *see winterreise*

der tod und das mädchen (vorüber ach vorüber!)
berlin   klust, piano   lp: dg LPEM 19 093-19 094
3-9   cd: dg 457 0182
march
1957

der wanderer (ich komme vom gebirge her)
berlin   klust, piano   lp: dg LPEM 19 093-19 094/LPEM 19 155
3-9   cd: dg 457 0182
march
1957

wasserflut *see winterreise*

der wegweiser *see winterreise*

die wetterfahne *see winterreise*

das wirtshaus *see winterreise*

josef greindl also recorded schubert lieder for the reichsrundfunk in 1943 and 1944 accompanied by michael raucheisen

HEINRICH SCHUETZ (1585-1672)

symphoniae sacrae: fili mi absalon; attendite
berlin instrumental 45: dg archiv EPA 37 012
17-19 ensemble
january
1954

ROBERT SCHUMANN (1810-1856)
josef greindl recorded one song, frühlingsfahrt, for the reichsrundfunk in 1943 accompanied by michael raucheisen

BEDRICH SMETANA (1824-1884)

the bartered bride, excerpt (just listen to me!)
munich *role of kecal* 45: dg EPL 30 554
2-6 **lehmann** lp: dg LPEM 19 014
february bavarian eadio lp: dg heliodor 89 637
1954 orchestra
 w.ludwig
 sung in german

GASPARO SPONTINI (1774-1851)
josef greindl took part in an unpublished reichsrundfunk recording of excerpts from la vestale conducted by robert heger

PIOTR TCHAIKOVSKY (1840-1893)

evgeny onegin, excerpt (everyone knows love on earth)
berlin *role of gremin* 45: dg EPL 30 102
11 february **lehmann** lp: dg LPEM 19 023
1954 rso berlin lp: dg heliodor 89 650
 sung in german

GIUSEPPE VERDI (1813-1901)

don carlo, excerpt (ella giammai m'amo)
berlin	*role of philip*	78: dg siemens LM 67 999
october-	**rother**	
november	städtische oper	
1942	orchestra	
	sung in german	

berlin	**lehmann**	78: dg LVM 72 482
11-14	rso berlin	45: dg EPL 30 078/EPL 30 268
february		lp: preiser 135021
1954		cd: preiser 90124

berlin	**lehmann**	78: dg LVM 72 481
11-14	rso berlin	45: dg EPL 30 077
february	*sung in german*	lp: dg LPE 17 014
1954		

josef greindl sings the role of king philip in a städtische oper performance of the opera conducted by ferenc fricsay and published by myto

la forza del destino, excerpt (son giunta!/madre pietosa vergine/infelice delusa rejetta!)
stuttgart	*role of guardino*	78: dg LVM 72 225-72 226
7-8	**leitner**	lp: dg LP 16 020/LPE 17 030
may	württem-	
1952	bergisches	
	staatsorchester	
	and chorus	
	kupper	
	neidlinger	

josef greindl also sings the role of padre guardino in an unpublished wdr cologne performance conducted by mario rossi

rigoletto
berlin   *role of sparafucile*   lp: dg LPEM 19 222-19 223
november   **heger**   lp: dg heliodor 89 026-89 027/2700 702
1944   staatskapelle   *originally a reichsrundfunk recording published by*
     and chorus   *urania and subsequently also issued by eterna,*
     berger   *saga (excerpts), basf/acanta and preiser*
     klose
     rosvaenge
     schlusnus
     hann
     sung in german

josef greindl also sings the bass part in a bavarian radio recording of the requiem conducted by eugen jochum and published by orfeo

RICHARD WAGNER (1813-1883)

der fliegende holländer
berlin   *role of daland*   lp: dg LPM 18 063-18 065/
october   **fricsay**   LPM 18 116-18 118
1952   rso berlin   lp: dg heliodor 89 753-89 755/2701 009
     rias choir   lp: decca (usa) DX 124
     kupper   cd: dg 439 7142/445 6872
     wagner   *excerpts*
     windgassen   45: dg EPL 30 024
     haefliger   lp: dg LPEM 19 122
     metternich   lp: dg heliodor 89 652

josef greindl sings the role of daland in two separate bayreuth festival performances conducted by wolfgang sawallisch and published by melodram and philips respectively

götterdämmerung, excerpt (hier sitz' ich zur wacht)
berlin	*role of hagen*	45: dg EPL 30 271
17 november	**ludwig**	lp: dg LPE 17 081/LPEM 19 063/
1955	rso berlin	2721 111
		lp: dg heliodor 89 800/478 438

götterdämmerung, excerpt (hoi ho ihr gibichsmannen!)
munich	*role of hagen*	78: dg LVM 72 224
3 february	**rieger**	lp: dg LPEM 19 042
1952	munich	
	philharmonic	
	bavarian state	
	opera chorus	

bayreuth	**pitz**	lp: dg LPEM 19 168/SLPEM 136 006/
22 august	bayreuth	2535 180/411 2461
1958	festival	
	orchestra	
	and chorus	

josef greindl sings the role of hagen in a total of seven bayreuth festival performances conducted variously by joseph keilberth, clemens krauss, hans knappertsbusch and karl böhm, and in a rai roma performance conducted by wilhelm furtwängler and published by emi and other labels

lohengrin, excerpt (gott grüss euch liebe männer von brabant!)
berlin	*role of heinrich*	78: dg siemens LM 67 975
november	**rother**	
1942	städtische oper	
	orchestra	

josef greindl sings the role of king heinrich in a wdr cologne performance of the opera conducted by richard kraus and published by movimento musica and myto, and in a bayreuth festival performance conducted by joseph keilberth and published by decca/teldec

Deutsche Grammophon Gesellschaft

Richard Wagner

RICHARD WAGNER
DIE WALKÜRE
Siegmund, sieh auf mich
GÖTTERDÄMMERUNG
Zu neuen Taten, teurer Helde (Duet)
Hier sitz' ich zur Wacht (Hagen's Vigil)

Astrid Varnay
Wolfgang Windgassen · Josef Greindl

Orchestra of the Bayreuther Festspiele
Conductor: Joseph Keilberth

LONG PLAYING RECORD
33⅓

DGM 19

die meistersinger von nürnberg, excerpt (das schöne fest johannistag)

berlin	*role of pogner*	78: dg siemens LM 67 975
november	**rother**	
1942	städtische oper orchestra	

berlin	**ludwig**	45: dg EPL 30 271
20 february	rso berlin	lp: dg LPE 17 081/2721 111
1956		lp: dg heliodor 2700 703
		cd: preiser 90124

josef greindl sings the role of pogner in bayreuth festival peformances conducted by wilhelm furtwängler, andré cluytens and erich leinsdorf and published on various labels

josef greindl also sings the role of hans sachs in a bayreuth festival performance conducted by hans knappertsbusch and published by melodram, also unpublished bayreuth festival performances conducted by josef krips and robert heger

parsifal, excerpt (titurel der fromme held)

stuttgart	*role of gurnemanz*	78: dg LV 36 074
22 april	**leitner**	45: dg NL 32 045
1952	württem- bergisches staatsorchester	lp: preiser 135021 cd: preiser 90124

parsifal, excerpt (von dorther kam das stöhnen/mich dünkt ich kenne diesen klageruf/heil dir mein gast!)

stuttgart	*role of gurnemanz*	lp: dg LPM 18 023
21-23	**leitner**	
april	württem-	
1952	bergisches staatsorchester	

parsifal, excerpt (das ist karfreitagszauber herr!)

stuttgart	*role of gurnemanz*	78: dg LVM 72 212
22 april	**leitner**	45: dg EPL 30 025
1952	württem- bergisches staatsorchester	lp: dg LPM 18 023/2721 115

josef greindl sings the role of gurnemanz in two bayreuth festival performances conducted by hans knappertsbusch published by melodram, and also the role of titurel in bayreuth festival perforamnces conducted by clemens krauss and hans knappertsbusch published by melodram and other labels

das rheingold
josef greindl sings the role of fafner in five bayreuth festival performances conducted variously by joseph keilberth, clemens krauss and hans knappertsbusch and issued on various labels; he sings the role of fasolt in a bayreuth festival performance conducted by hans knappertsbusch and issued by melodram and music and arts, and in a rai roma performance conducted by wilhelm furtwängler issued by emi and other labels

siegfried
josef greindl sings the role of fafner in four bayreuth festival performances conducted variously by clemens krauss, joseph keilberth and hans knappertsbusch, and in a rai roma performance conducted by wilhelm furtwängler and issued by emi and other labels

tannhäuser, excerpt (gar viel und schön)
berlin	*role of landgraf*	45: dg NL 32 116
17-18	**ludwig**	lp: dg LPEM 19 069/2721 111
november	rso berlin	lp: preiser 135021
1955		cd: preiser 90124

josef greindl sings the role of landgraf hermann in a berlin städtische oper performance conducted by leopold ludwig and published by gebhardt, and in bayreuth festival performances conducted by joseph keilberth and wolfgang sawallisch and published on various labels

tristan und isolde
josef greindl sings the role of marke in the emi recording conducted by wilhelm furtwängler and in a bayreuth festival performance conducted by karl böhm and published by melodram

die walküre, act one

stuttgart	*role of hunding*	lp: dg LPM 18 022-18 023
17-20	**leitner**	lp: dg heliodor 2548 735
november	württem-	lp: decca (usa) DX 121
1951	bergisches	cd: dg eloquence awaiting publication
	staatsorchester	*excerpts*
	müller	78: dg LV 36 053
	windgassen	45: dg EPL 30 031/EPL 30 501

josef greindl also sings hunding in a vienna festival concert performance of act one conducted by hans knappertsbusch and published by living stage (it also exists as an unpublished video recording from austrian television)

josef greindl sings the role of hunding in a total of eight bayreuth festival performamces conducted variously by joseph keilberth, clemens krauss and hans knappertsbusch, and also in a berlin städtische oper performance conducted by ferenc fricsay and published by myto

CARL MARIA VON WEBER (1786-1826)

der freischütz, kurzoper

berlin	*role of eremit*	78: dg siemens LM 68 074-68 081
1943	**heger**	lp: decca (usa) DX 112
	städtische oper	*greindl is heard only on record LM 68 080*
	orchestra	
	staatsoper chorus	
	müller	
	spletter	
	seider	
	hann	
	grossmann	
	domgraf-fassbänder	

kim borg
1919-2000

JOHANN SEBASTIAN BACH (1685-1750)
kim borg is bass soloist in a philips recording of mass in b minor conducted by eugen jochum

LUDWIG VAN BEETHOVEN (1770-1827)

die ehre gottes in der natur/gellert-lieder
copenhagen   wöldike, organ   45: dg NL 32 104
1953   *danish radio recording*

flohlied (es war einmal ein könig)
munich   werba, piano   45: dg NL 32 228
7 june
1956

ALEXANDER BORODIN (1833-1887)

prince igor, excerpt (no sleep no rest)
berlin   *role of igor*   lp: dg LPEM 19 386/SLPEM 136 386/
2-5   **stein**   135 090
january   rso berlin   cd: finlandia 4509 956062
1963

prince igor, excerpt (how goes it prince?)
berlin   *role of konchak*   lp: dg LPEM 19 386/SLPEM 136 386/
2-5   **stein**   135 090
january   rso berlin   cd: finlandia 4509 956062
1963

RUSSISCHE OPERN-ARIEN

Chowantschina · Boris Godunow · Eugen Onegin
Das Leben für den Zaren · Fürst Igor

KIM BORG

JOHANNES BRAHMS (1833-1897)

vier ernste gesänge: denn es gehet dem menschen wie dem vieh; ich wandte mich und sahe an alle; o tod wie bitter bist du; wenn ich mit menschen- und mit engelszungen redete

vienna	werba, piano	lp: dg LPEM 19 163/SLPEM 136 015
29 may-		cd: finlandia 4509 956062
7 june		
1958		

ANTON BRUCKNER (1824-1896)

mass no 3

munich	*bass soloist*	lp: dg LPM 18 829/SLPM 138 829/
4-6	**jochum**	2720 054
july	bavarian radio	cd: dg 423 1272/447 4092
1962	orchestra	
	and chorus	
	stader	
	hellmann	
	haefliger	

kim borg also sings the bass part in a bavarian radio recording of the te deum conducted by eugen jochum and published by orfeo

ANTONIN DVORAK (1841-1904)

requiem
prague 　　　*bass soloist*　　　lp: dg LPM 18 547-18 548/
30 january-　　**ancerl**　　　　　　　SLPM 138 026-138 027/2707 005
4 february　　czech　　　　　　cd: dg 437 3772
1959　　　　　philharmonic　　*probably also published on the supraphon label*
　　　　　　　orchestra
　　　　　　　and chorus
　　　　　　　stader
　　　　　　　wagner
　　　　　　　haefliger

stabat mater
prague　　　　*bass soloist*　　　lp: dg LPM 18 818-18 819/
15-20　　　　**smetacek**　　　　　　SLPM 138 818-138 819/2707 014
december　　czech　　　　　　*probably also published on the supraphon label*
1961　　　　　philharmonic
　　　　　　　orchestra
　　　　　　　and chorus
　　　　　　　woytowicz
　　　　　　　soukoupova
　　　　　　　zidek

EDWARD ELGAR (1857-1934)
kim borg sings the parts of priest and angel of the agony in the dream of gerontius conducted by sir john barbirolli and published by emi

MIKHAIL GLINKA (1804-1857)

a life for the tsar, excerpt (they sense the truth!)
berlin　　　　*role of susanin*　　lp: dg LPEM 19 386/SLPEM 136 386/
2-5　　　　　**stein**　　　　　　　　135 090
january　　　rso berlin　　　　cd: finlandia 4509 956062
1963

CHARLES GOUNOD (1818-1893)

faust, excerpt (le veau d'or)
munich   *role of mephisto*   45: dg EPL 30 339
12 january   **leitner**   cd: dg 449 9262
1957   munich
                philharmonic
                bavarian radio
                chorus

munich   **leitner**   45: dg EPL 30 338
12 january   munich   lp: dg LPEM 19 095
1957   philharmonic   lp: dg heliodor 89 651
                bavarian radio
                chorus
                sung in german

faust, excerpt (vous qui faites l'endormie)
munich   *role of mephisto*   45: dg EPL 30 339
10 january   **leitner**   cd: dg 449 9262
1957   munich
                philharmonic

munich   **leitner**   45: dg EPL 30 338
10 january   munich   lp: dg LPEM 19 095
1957   philharmonic   lp: dg heliodor 89 651
                sung in german

faust, excerpt (alerte! alerte!)
munich   *role of mephisto*   lp: dg LPEM 19 095
11-12   **leitner**   lp: dg heliodor 89 651
january   munich
1957   philharmonic
                bavarian radio
                chorus
                stader
                hoppe
                sung in german

GEORGE FRIDERIC HANDEL (1685-1759)

arioso (dank sei dir herr!)
copenhagen   wöldike, organ   45: dg NL 32 104
1953   *danish radio recording*

FRANZ JOSEF HAYDN (1732-1809)

die schöpfung
berlin	*bass soloist*	lp: dg NK 551-553/AK 561-563/
6-11	**markevitch**	LPM 18 489-18 490
may	berlin	lp: dg heliodor 2700 105
1955	philharmonic	lp: decca (usa) DX 138
	saint hedwig's	cd: dg 437 3802
	choir	
	seefried	
	holm	

YRJO KILPINEN (1892-1959)

songs: somm ett blommande m andelträd; om tiotusen ar
vienna   werba, piano   lp: dg LPM 18 592/SLPM 138 060
1-4   cd: finlandia 4509 956062
june
1959
kim borg also recorded a recital of kilpinen lieder for philips, accompanied by pentti koskimies

CARL LOEWE (1796-1869)

hochzeitlied (wir singen und sagen)
hannover	raucheisen,	lp: dg LPE 17 004
25-28	piano	cd: finlandia 4509 956062
april		
1953		

kleiner haushalt (einen haushalt klein und fein)
hannover	raucheisen,	lp: dg LPE 17 004
25-28	piano	cd: finlandia 4509 956062
april		
1953		

ALBERT LORTZING (1801-1851)

der waffenschmied, excerpt (auch ich war ein jüngling mit lockigem haar)
munich	*role of stadinger*	45: dg EPL 30 108
15 april	**leitner**	lp: dg LPE 17 093
1955	munich	cd: dg 449 9262
	philharmonic	

WOLFGANG AMADEUS MOZART (1756-1791)

concert arias: mentre ti lascio o figlia; per quella bella mano
munich	**leitner**	45: dg EPL 30 092
16-17	munich	lp: dg LPM 18 219
october	philharmonic	
1954		

die zauberflöte
berlin   *roles of sprecher*   lp: dg LPM 18 264-18 266/
june   *and second*   LPM 18 267-18 269/2728 009
1955   *armed man*   lp: dg heliodor 89 662-89 664/
                fricsay   2701 003/2730 014
                rso berlin   lp: decca (usa) DX 134
                rias choir   lp: philips 6747 387
                stader   lp: eterna 820 226-820 228
                streich   cd: dg 437 7412/459 4972
                otto   *excerpts*
                schech   lp: dg LPM 18 558-18 559
                klose
                haefliger
                fischer-dieskau
                greindl

die zauberflöte, excerpt (o isis und osiris)
munich   *role of sarastro*   78: dg LV 36 089
18 june   **rother**   lp: dg LPE 17 093
1953   munich   cd: dg 449 9262
                philharmonic   cd: finlandia 4509 956062
                bavarian radio
                chorus

die zauberflöte, excerpt (in diesen heil'gen hallen)
munich   *role of sarastro*   78: dg LV 36 089
18 june   **rother**   45: dg EPL 30 011
1953   munich   cd: dg 449 9262
                philharmonic   cd: finlandia 4509 956062

kim borg *bass*

MUSSORGSKY
"Boris Godunov"
Pimenn's Monologue

ROSSINI
"The Barber of Seville"
La Calumnia

Deutsche Grammophon Gesellschaft

45
30 075 EPL

requiem mass
vienna	*bass soloist*	lp: dg archiv APM 14 111-14 112
29 november-	**jochum**	lp: dg NK 504-505/LPM 18 284
2 december	vienna	lp: dg heliodor 89 508
1955	symphony	lp: decca (usa) DL 8935
	vienna opera	lp: heliodor (usa) H 25000/HS 25000
	chorus	cd: dg 437 3892
	seefried	*APM 14 111-14 112 and NK 504-505*
	pitzinger	*also included liturgy of the service in stephansdom*
	holm	*at which the performance was recorded, on the eve of the mozart bi-centenary celebrations*

MODEST MUSSORGSKY (1839-1881)

boris godunov, excerpt (i have attained the highest power)
berlin	*title role*	lp: dg LPEM 19 386/SLPEM 136 386/
2-5	**stein**	135 090
january	rso berlin	cd: finlandia 4509 956062
1963		

boris godunov, excerpt (death of boris)
berlin	*title role*	lp: dg LPEM 19 386/SLPEM 136 386/
2-5	**stein**	135 090
january	rso berlin	cd: finlandia 4509 956062
1963	rias choir	

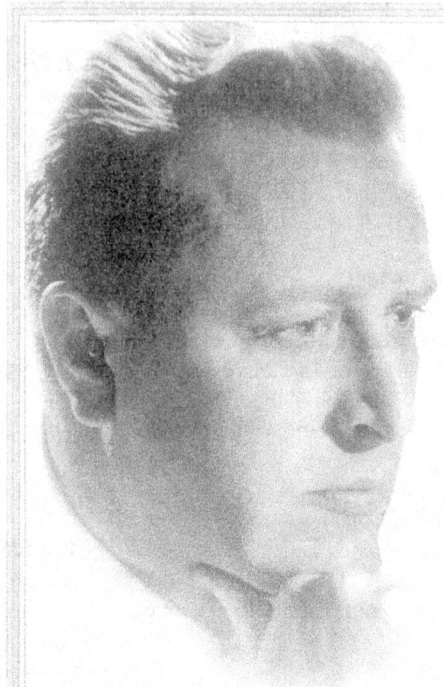

boris godunov, excerpt (yet one last tale)
munich	*role of pimen*	78: dg LV 36 095
17-21	**rother**	45: dg EPL 30 075
june	munich	
1953	philharmonic	

munich	**rother**	78: dg LV 36 008
17-21	munich	45: dg EPL 30 019
june	philharmonic	
1953	*sung in german*	

berlin	**stein**	lp: dg LPEM 19 386/SLPEM 136 386/
2-5	rso berlin	135 090
january		cd: finlandia 4509 956062
1963		

kim borg sings the roles of shchelkalov and rangoni in the emi recording of boris godunov conducted by issay dobrowen

khovantschina, excerpt (here on this spot)
berlin	*role of dosifei*	lp: dg LPEM 19 386/SLPEM 136 386/
2-5	**stein**	135 090
january	rso berlin	cd: finlandia 4509 956062
1963		

songs and dances of death: lullaby; serenade; trepak; the field marshal
munich	werba, piano	lp: dg LPEM 19 076
5-7	*sung in german*	cd: finlandia 4509 956062
june		
1956		

kim borg also performs the orchestral version of these songs conducted by eugen jochum and published by tahra

the classicist
munich	werba, piano	lp: dg LPEM 19 076
5-7	*sung in german*	
june		
1956		

the fiddler's song
munich	werba, piano	lp: dg LPEM 19 076
5-7	*sung in german*	
june		
1956		

the field marshal *see songs and dances of death*

the garden by the don
munich	werba, piano	lp: dg LPEM 19 076
5-7	*sung in german*	
june		
1956		

vienna	werba, piano	lp: dg LPM 18 592/SLPM 138 060
1-4		cd: finlandia 4509 956062
june		
1959		

lullaby *see songs and dances of death*

mephisto's song of the flea
munich	werba, piano	45: dg NL 32 228
5-7	*sung in german*	lp: dg LPEM 19 076
june		
1956		

vienna	werba, piano	lp: dg LPM 18 592/SLPM 138 060
1-4		cd: finlandia 4509 956062
june		
1959		

the seminarist
munich	werba, piano	lp: dg LPEM 19 076
5-7		
june		
1956		

256

serenade *see songs and dances of death*

trepak *see songs and dances of death*

where art thou little star?
munich 5-7 june 1956	werba, piano *sung in german*	lp: dg LPEM 19 076

vienna 1-4 june 1959	werba, piano	lp: dg LPM 18 592/SLPM 138 060 cd: finlandia 4509 956062

kim borg also recorded mussorgsky songs with piano and orchestra for the supraphon label

OTTO NICOLAI (1810-1849)

die lustigen weiber von windsor, excerpt (als büblein klein)
munich 15 april 1955	*role of falstaff* **leitner** munich philharmonic bavarian radio chorus	45: dg EPL 30 108 lp: dg LPEM 19 049 lp: dg heliodor 89 648 cd: dg 449 9262

die lustigen weiber von windsor, excerpt (in einem waschkorb?)
munich 14 april 1955	*role of falstaff* **leitner** munich philharmonic wächter	45: dg EPL 30 277 lp: dg LPEM 19 049 lp: dg heliodor 89 648 lp: preiser 135015 cd: preiser 90346

CARL ORFF (1895-1982)

antigonae

munich	*role of messenger*	lp: dg 2709 009/2740 226
25 march-	**leitner**	cd: dg 437 7212
16 april	bavarian radio	
1961	orchestra	
	and chorus	
	borkh	
	plümacher	
	hellmann	
	stolze	
	haefliger	
	uhl	
	alexander	

GIACOMO PUCCINI

Madame Butterfly

in deutsch gesungen

Anny Schlemm · Sándor Kónya · Kim Borg

Dirigent: Ferdinand Leitner

Deutsche Grammophon Gesellschaft

REPRÄSENTATIVE AUSZÜGE AUS UNSEREM OPERNREPERTOIRE
(540) HI-FI

GIACOMO PUCCINI (1858-1924)

madama butterfly
stuttgart *role of sharpless* lp: dg LPM 18 750-18 752/
28 february- **leitner** SLPM 138 750-138 752
8 march württem- *excerpts*
1961 bergisches lp: dg LPEM 19 401/SLPEM 136 401/
staatsorchester 2537 011
and chorus
schlemm
plümacher
konya
sung in german

tosca, excerpt (tre sbirri!)
berlin *role of scarpia* lp: dg LPEM 19 403/SLPEM 136 403
1960 **stein**
staatskapelle
and chorus
komische oper
chorus
sung in german

tosca, excerpt (odi? e il tamburo!/vissi d'arte)
berlin *role of scarpia* lp: dg LPEM 19 403/SLPEM 136 403
1960 **stein**
staatskapelle
woytowicz
sung in german

GIOACCHINO ROSSINI (1792-1868)

stabat mater
berlin	*bass soloist*	lp: dg LPM 18 203-18 204/LPM 18 340/
16-19	**fricsay**	2535 718
september	rso berlin	lp: dg heliodor 89 610/2548 126
1954	rias choir	lp: decca (usa) DX 132
	stader	cd: dg 439 6842
	radev	
	haefliger	

il barbiere di siviglia, excerpt (la calunnia e un venticello)
munich	*role of basilio*	78: dg LV 36 095
21 june	**rother**	45: dg EPL 30 075
1953	munich	cd: dg 449 9262
	philharmonic	cd: finlandia 4509 956062

munich	**rother**	78: dg LV 36 088
21 june	munich	45: dg EPL 30 019
1953	philharmonic	
	sung in german	

berlin	**peters**	lp: dg LPEM 19 423/SLPEM 136 423/
20-24	deutsche oper	2535 374
april	orchestra	
1964	*sung in german*	

il barbiere di siviglia, excerpt (amor e fede eterna!)
berlin	*role of basilio*	lp: dg LPEM 19 423/SLPEM 136 423/
20-24	**peters**	2535 374
april	deutsche oper	
1964	orchestra	
	rias choir	
	streich	
	haefliger	
	grumbach	
	sardi	
	sung in german	

FRANZ SCHUBERT (1797-1828)

an die leier (ich will von atreus söhnen)
hannover   raucheisen,   lp: dg LPE 17 004
25-28   piano
april
1953

erlkönig (wer reiter so spät durch nacht und wind?)
vienna   werba, piano   lp: dg LPM 18 592/SLPM 138 060
1-4   cd: finlandia 4509 956062
june
1959

gesänge des harfners: wer sich der einsamkeit ergibt; wer nie sein brot mit tränen ass; an die türen will ich schleichen
vienna   werba, piano   lp: dg LPEM 19 163/SLPEM 136 015
29 may-   cd: finlandia 4509 956062
7 june
1958

grenzen der menschheit (wenn der uralte heilige vater)
hannover   raucheisen,   lp: dg LPE 17 004
25-28   piano
april
1953

der könig in thule (es war ein könig in thule)
hannover   raucheisen,   lp: dg LPE 17 004
25-28   piano   cd: finlandia 4509 956062
april
1953

prometheus (bedecke deinen himmel zeus!)
vienna   werba, piano   lp: dg LPM 18 592/SLPM 138 060
1-4   cd: finlandia 4509 956062
june
1959

ROBERT SCHUMANN (1810-1856)

die beiden grenadiere (nach frankreich zogen zwei grenadier')
hannover   raucheisen,   lp: dg LPE 17 004
25-28   piano   cd: finlandia 4509 956062
april
1953

JEAN SIBELIUS (1865-1957)

songs: lastu lainehilla; illale; sonda sonda sinisorsa; finlandia-hymni; drömmen; varen flyktar hastigt; till frigga; flagellek; romeo; demanten pa marssnön; säv säv susa; svarta rosor
munich   werba, piano   lp: dg LPEM 19 113
27-29   cd: finlandia 4509 956062
may   *recordings completed in june 1957*
1957

2 songs from shakespeare's twelfth night: come away death; when i was a little tiny boy
munich   werba, piano   lp: dg LPEM 19 113
27-29
may
1957

les trois soeurs aveugles
munich   werba, piano   lp: dg LPEM 19 113
27-29
may
1957

im feld ein mädchen singt
munich   werba, piano   lp: dg LPEM 19 113
27-29
may
1957

PIOTR TCHAIKOVSKY (1840-1893)

evgeny onegin, excerpt (everyone knows love on earth)
berlin	*role of gremin*	lp: dg LPEM 19 386/SLPEM 136 386/
2-5	**stein**	135 090
january	rso berlin	cd: finlandia 4509 956062
1963		

kim borg also recorded a group of tchaikovsky songs for the supraphon label

GIUSEPPE VERDI (1813-1901)

messsa da requiem
berlin	*bass soloist*	lp: dg LPM 18 155-18 156/
22-26	**fricsay**	LPM 18 157-18 158
september	rso berlin	lp: decca (usa) DX 118
1953	rias and saint	cd: dg 447 4422
	hedwig's choirs	
	stader	
	radev	
	krebs	

kim borg also takes part in an unpublished swedish radio recording of the requiem conducted by sixten ehrling

don carlo, excerpt (ella giammai m'amo)
munich	*role of philip*	45: dg EPL 30 268
17-19	**rother**	cd: dg 449 9262
november	bamberg so	cd: finlandia 4509 956062
1955		

munich	**rother**	45: dg EPL 30 267
17-19	bamberg so	lp: dg LPE 17 093
november	*sung in german*	
1955		

nabucco, excerpt (oh chi piange?)
munich	*role of zaccaria*	78: dg LM 68 475
18 november	**rother**	45: dg EPL 30 125/NL 32 314
1955	bamberg so	cd: dg 449 9262
	bavarian radio	
	chorus	
	sung in german	

simon boccanegra, excerpt (il lacerato spirito)
munich	*role of fiesco*	45: dg EPL 30 236
17-19	**rother**	cd: dg 449 9262
november	bamberg so	
1955	bavarian radio	
	chorus	

munich	**rother**	45: dg EPL 30 235
17-19	bamberg so	lp: dg LPE 17 093
november	bavarian radio	
1955	chorus	
	sung in german	

i vespri siciliani, excerpt (o tu palermo)
munich	*role of arrigo*	45: dg EPL 30 236
17-19	**rother**	cd: dg 449 9262
november	bamberg so	
1955		

munich	**rother**	45: dg EPL 30 235
17-19	bamberg so	lp: dg LPE 17 093
november	*sung in german*	
1955		

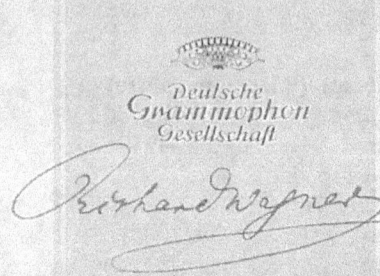

RICHARD WAGNER (1813-1883)

der fliegende holländer, excerpt (mögst du mein kind)
bamberg	*role of daland*	lp: dg LPEM 19 425/SLPEM 136 425
10-11	**löwlein**	*recording completed in august 1964*
july	bamberg so	
1964	stewart	

der fliegende holländer, excerpt (verloren ach verloren!)
bamberg	*role of daland*	lp: dg LPEM 19 425/SLPEM 136 425/
10-11	**löwlein**	135 150
july	bamberg so	*recording completed in august 1964*
1964	deutsche oper	
	chorus	
	lear	
	king	
	stewart	

tristan und isolde, excerpt (tatest du's wirklich?)
munich	*role of marke*	lp: dg LPEM 19 018
18 october	**leitner**	lp: decca (usa) DL 9897
1954	munich	cd: dg 449 9262
	philharmonic	

HUGO WOLF (1860-1903)

abschied/mörike-lieder
vienna	werba, piano	lp: dg LPM 18 592/SLPM 138 060
1-4		cd: finlandia 4509 956062
june		
1959		

michelangelo-lieder: wohl denk' ich oft; alles endet was entsteht; fühlt meine seele
vienna	werba, piano	lp: dg LPEM 19 163/SLPEM 136 015
29 may-		cd: finlandia 4509 956062
7 june		
1958		

der tambour/mörike-lieder
vienna	werba, piano	lp: dg LPM 18 592/SLPM 138 060
1-4		cd: finlandia 4509 956062
june		
1959		

zur warnung/mörike-lieder
vienna	werba, piano	lp: dg LPM 18 592/SLPM 138 060
1-4		cd: finlandia 4509 956062
june		
1959		

Discographies by Travis & Emery:

Discographies by John Hunt.

1987: From Adam to Webern: the Recordings of von Karajan.
1991: 3 Italian Conductors and 7 Viennese Sopranos: 10 Discographies: Arturo Toscanini, Guido Cantelli, Carlo Maria Giulini, Elisabeth Schwarzkopf, Irmgard Seefried, Elisabeth Gruemmer, Sena Jurinac, Hilde Gueden, Lisa Della Casa, Rita Streich.
1992: Mid-Century Conductors and More Viennese Singers: 10 Discographies: Karl Boehm, Victor De Sabata, Hans Knappertsbusch, Tullio Serafin, Clemens Krauss, Anton Dermota, Leonie Rysanek, Eberhard Waechter, Maria Reining, Erich Kunz.
1993: More 20th Century Conductors: 7 Discographies: Eugen Jochum, Ferenc Fricsay, Carl Schuricht, Felix Weingartner, Josef Krips, Otto Klemperer, Erich Kleiber.
1994: Giants of the Keyboard: 6 Discographies: Wilhelm Kempff, Walter Gieseking, Edwin Fischer, Clara Haskil, Wilhelm Backhaus, Artur Schnabel.
1994: Six Wagnerian Sopranos: 6 Discographies: Frieda Leider, Kirsten Flagstad, Astrid Varnay, Martha Moedl, Birgit Nilsson, Gwyneth Jones.
1995: Musical Knights: 6 Discographies: Henry Wood, Thomas Beecham, Adrian Boult, John Barbirolli, Reginald Goodall, Malcolm Sargent.
1995: A Notable Quartet: 4 Discographies: Gundula Janowitz, Christa Ludwig, Nicolai Gedda, Dietrich Fischer-Dieskau.
1996: The Post-War German Tradition: 5 Discographies: Rudolf Kempe, Joseph Keilberth, Wolfgang Sawallisch, Rafael Kubelik, Andre Cluytens.
1996: Teachers and Pupils: 7 Discographies: Elisabeth Schwarzkopf, Maria Ivoguen, Maria Cebotari, Meta Seinemeyer, Ljuba Welitsch, Rita Streich, Erna Berger.
1996: Tenors in a Lyric Tradition: 3 Discographies: Peter Anders, Walther Ludwig, Fritz Wunderlich.
1997: The Lyric Baritone: 5 Discographies: Hans Reinmar, Gerhard Hüsch, Josef Metternich, Hermann Uhde, Eberhard Wächter.
1997: Hungarians in Exile: 3 Discographies: Fritz Reiner, Antal Dorati, George Szell.
1997: The Art of the Diva: 3 Discographies: Claudia Muzio, Maria Callas, Magda Olivero.
1997: Metropolitan Sopranos: 4 Discographies: Rosa Ponselle, Eleanor Steber, Zinka Milanov, Leontyne Price.
1997: Back From The Shadows: 4 Discographies: Willem Mengelberg, Dimitri Mitropoulos, Hermann Abendroth, Eduard Van Beinum.
1997: More Musical Knights: 4 Discographies: Hamilton Harty, Charles Mackerras, Simon Rattle, John Pritchard.
1998: Conductors On The Yellow Label: 8 Discographies: Fritz Lehmann, Ferdinand Leitner, Ferenc Fricsay, Eugen Jochum, Leopold Ludwig, Artur Rother, Franz Konwitschny, Igor Markevitch.
1998: More Giants of the Keyboard: 5 Discographies: Claudio Arrau, Gyorgy Cziffra, Vladimir Horowitz, Dinu Lipatti, Artur Rubinstein.

1998: Mezzos and Contraltos. 5 Discographies: Janet Baker, Margarete Klose, Kathleen Ferrier, Giulietta Simionato, Elisabeth Höngen.
1999: The Furtwängler Sound Sixth Edition: Discography and Concert Listing.
1999: The Great Dictators: 3 Discographies: Evgeny Mravinsky, Artur Rodzinski, Sergiu Celibidache.
1999: Sviatoslav Richter: Pianist of the Century: Discography.
2000: Philharmonic Autocrat 1: Discography of: Herbert Von Karajan [Third Edition].
2000: Wiener Philharmoniker 1 - Vienna Philharmonic & Vienna State Opera Orchestras: Disc. Part 1 1905-1954.
2000: Wiener Philharmoniker 2 - Vienna Philharmonic & Vienna State Opera Orchestras: Disc. Part 2 1954-1989.
2001: Gramophone Stalwarts: 3 Separate Discographies: Bruno Walter, Erich Leinsdorf, Georg Solti.
2001: Singers of the Third Reich: 5 Discographies: Helge Roswaenge, Tiana Lemnitz, Franz Völker, Maria Müller, Max Lorenz.
2001: Philharmonic Autocrat 2: Concert Register of Herbert Von Karajan Second Edition.
2002: Sächsische Staatskapelle Dresden: Complete Discography.
2002: Carlo Maria Giulini: Discography and Concert Register.
2002: Pianists For The Connoisseur: 6 Discographies: Arturo Benedetti Michelangeli, Alfred Cortot, Alexis Weissenberg, Clifford Curzon, Solomon, Elly Ney.
2003: Singers on the Yellow Label: 7 Discographies: Maria Stader, Elfriede Trötschel, Annelies Kupper, Wolfgang Windgassen, Ernst Häfliger, Josef Greindl, Kim Borg.
2003: A Gallic Trio: 3 Discographies: Charles Münch, Paul Paray, Pierre Monteux.
2004: Antal Dorati 1906-1988: Discography and Concert Register.
2004: Columbia 33CX Label Discography.
2004: Great Violinists: 3 Discographies: David Oistrakh, Wolfgang Schneiderhan, Arthur Grumiaux.
2006: Leopold Stokowski: Second Edition of the Discography.
2006: Wagner Im Festspielhaus: Discography of the Bayreuth Festival.
2006: Her Master's Voice: Concert Register and Discography of Dame Elisabeth Schwarzkopf [Third Edition].
2007: Hans Knappertsbusch: Kna: Concert Register and Discography of Hans Knappertsbusch, 1888-1965. Second Edition.
2008: Philips Minigroove: Second Extended Version of the European Discography.
2009: American Classics: The Discographies of Leonard Bernstein and Eugene Ormandy.

Discography by Stephen J. Pettitt, edited by John Hunt:
1987: Philharmonia Orchestra: Complete Discography 1945-1987

Available from: Travis & Emery at 17 Cecil Court, London, UK. (+44) 20 7 240 2129. email on sales@travis-and-emery.com .

© Travis & Emery 2009

Music and Books published by Travis & Emery Music Bookshop:

Anon.: Hymnarium Sarisburense, cum Rubris et Notis Musicus
Agricola, Johann Friedrich from Tosi: Anleitung zur Singkunst. (Faksimile 1757)
Bach, C.P.E.: edited W. Emery: Nekrolog or Obituary Notice of J.S. Bach.
Bateson, Naomi Judith: Alcock of Salisbury
Bathe, William: A Briefe Introduction to the Skill of Song
Bax, Arnold: Symphony #5, Arranged for Piano Four Hands by Walter Emery
Burney, Charles: The Present State of Music in France and Italy
Burney, Charles: The Present State of Music in Germany, The Netherlands …
Burney, Charles: An Account of the Musical Performances … Handel
Burney, Karl: Nachricht von Georg Friedrich Handel's Lebensumstanden.
Burns, Robert (jnr): The Caledonian Musical Museum (1810 volume)
Cobbett, W.W.: Cobbett's Cyclopedic Survey of Chamber Music. (2 vols.)
Corrette, Michel: Le Maitre de Clavecin
Crimp, Bryan: Dear Mr. Rosenthal … Dear Mr. Gaisberg …
Crimp, Bryan: Solo: The Biography of Solomon
d'Indy, Vincent: Beethoven: Biographie Critique
d'Indy, Vincent: Beethoven: A Critical Biography
d'Indy, Vincent: César Franck (in French)
Fischhof, Joseph: Versuch einer Geschichte des Clavierbaues
Frescobaldi, Girolamo: D'Arie Musicali per Cantarsi. Primo Libro & Secondo Libro.
Geminiani, Francesco: The Art of Playing the Violin.
Handel; Purcell; Boyce; Green et al: Calliope or English Harmony: Volume First.
Hawkins, John: A General History of the Science and Practice of Music (5 vols.)
Herbert-Caesari, Edgar: The Science and Sensations of Vocal Tone
Herbert-Caesari, Edgar: Vocal Truth
Hopkins and Rimboult: The Organ. Its History and Construction.
Hunt, John: some 40 discographies – see list of discographies
Isaacs, Lewis: Hänsel and Gretel. A Guide to Humperdinck's Opera.
Isaacs, Lewis: Königskinder (Royal Children) A Guide to Humperdinck's Opera.
Lacassagne, M. l'Abbé Joseph : Traité Général des élémens du Chant.
Lascelles (née Catley), Anne: The Life of Miss Anne Catley.
Mainwaring, John: Memoirs of the Life of the Late George Frederic Handel
Malcolm, Alexander: A Treaty of Music: Speculative, Practical and Historical
Marx, Adolph Bernhard: Die Kunst des Gesanges, Theoretisch-Practisch
May, Florence: The Life of Brahms
Mellers, Wilfrid: Angels of the Night: Popular Female Singers of Our Time
Mellers, Wilfrid: Bach and the Dance of God

Travis & Emery Music Bookshop
17 Cecil Court, London, WC2N 4EZ, United Kingdom.
Tel. (+44) 20 7240 2129

Music and Books published by Travis & Emery Music Bookshop:
Mellers, Wilfrid: Beethoven and the Voice of God
Mellers, Wilfrid: Caliban Reborn - Renewal in Twentieth Century Music
Mellers, Wilfrid: François Couperin and the French Classical Tradition
Mellers, Wilfrid: Harmonious Meeting
Mellers, Wilfrid: Le Jardin Retrouvé, The Music of Frederic Mompou
Mellers, Wilfrid: Music and Society, England and the European Tradition
Mellers, Wilfrid: Music in a New Found Land: …… American Music
Mellers, Wilfrid: Romanticism and the Twentieth Century (from 1800)
Mellers, Wilfrid: The Masks of Orpheus: …… the Story of European Music.
Mellers, Wilfrid: The Sonata Principle (from c. 1750)
Mellers, Wilfrid: Vaughan Williams and the Vision of Albion
Panchianio, Cattuffio: Rutzvanscad Il Giovine.
Pearce, Charles: Sims Reeves, Fifty Years of Music in England.
Pettitt, Stephen: Philharmonia Orchestra: Complete Discography 1945-1987
Playford, John: An Introduction to the Skill of Musick.
Purcell, Henry et al: Harmonia Sacra … The First Book, (1726)
Purcell, Henry et al: Harmonia Sacra … Book II (1726)
Quantz, Johann: Versuch einer Anweisung die Flöte traversiere zu spielen.
Rameau, Jean-Philippe: Code de Musique Pratique, ou Methodes.
Rastall, Richard: The Notation of Western Music.
Rimbault, Edward: The Pianoforte, Its Origins, Progress, and Construction.
Rousseau, Jean Jacques: Dictionnaire de Musique
Rubinstein, Anton : Guide to the proper use of the Pianoforte Pedals.
Sainsbury, John S.: Dictionary of Musicians. Vol. 1. (1825). 2 vols.
Simpson, Christopher: A Compendium of Practical Musick in Five Parts
Spohr, Louis: Autobiography
Spohr, Louis: Grand Violin School
Tans'ur, William: A New Musical Grammar; or The Harmonical Spectator
Terry, Charles Sanford: Four-Part Chorals of J.S. Bach. (German & English)
Terry, Charles Sanford: Joh. Seb. Bach, Cantata Texts, Sacred and Secular.
Terry, Charles Sanford: The Origins of the Family of Bach Musicians.
Tosi, Pierfrancesco: Opinioni de' Cantori Antichi, e Moderni
Van der Straeten, Edmund: History of the Violoncello, The Viol da Gamba …
Van der Straeten, Edmund: History of the Violin, Its Ancestors… (2 vols.)
Walther, J. G.: Musicalisches Lexikon ober Musicalische Bibliothec (1732)

Travis & Emery Music Bookshop
17 Cecil Court, London, WC2N 4EZ, United Kingdom.
Tel. (+44) 20 7240 2129

© Travis & Emery 2009

www.ingramcontent.com/pod-product-compliance
Lightning Source LLC
Chambersburg PA
CBHW071833230426
43671CB00012B/1946